THE AFTERMATH OF THE BATTLE OF LITTLE BIG HORN

"I regard Custer's massacre as an unnecessary sacrifice
of troops brought on by Custer himself"

President U.S. Grant (1822–1885)

THE AFTERMATH OF THE BATTLE OF LITTLE BIG HORN

WENDY ANN WALLACE

Pen & Sword
MILITARY
AN IMPRINT OF PEN & SWORD BOOKS LTD.
YORKSHIRE – PHILADELPHIA

First published in Great Britain in 2023 by
PEN AND SWORD MILITARY
An imprint of
Pen & Sword Books Limited
Yorkshire – Philadelphia

ISBN 978 1 39904 676 3

A CIP catalogue record for this book is available from the British Library.

Typeset in Times New Roman 11/13.5 by
SJmagic DESIGN SERVICES, India.
Printed and bound in the UK by CPI Group (UK) Ltd.

Pen & Sword Books Limited incorporates the imprints of Atlas, Archaeology, Aviation, Discovery, Family History, Fiction, History, Maritime, Military, Military Classics, Politics, Select, Transport, True Crime, Air World, Frontline Publishing, Leo Cooper, Remember When, Seaforth Publishing, The Praetorian Press, Wharncliffe Local History, Wharncliffe Transport, Wharncliffe True Crime and White Owl.

For a complete list of Pen & Sword titles please contact
PEN & SWORD BOOKS LIMITED
George House, Units 12 & 13, Beevor Street, Off Pontefract Road,
Barnsley, South Yorkshire, S71 1HN, England
E-mail: enquiries@pen-and-sword.co.uk
Website: www.pen-and-sword.co.uk

or

PEN AND SWORD BOOKS
1950 Lawrence Rd, Havertown, PA 19083, USA
E-mail: uspen-and-sword@casematepublishers.com
Website: www.penandswordbooks.com

MIX
Paper | Supporting responsible forestry
FSC® C013604

For Hayley

Also available from Pen & Sword Books:
The Battle of the Little Big Horn: A New Appraisal

Contents

Author's Note

Conspirators and murderers generally do not leave a paper trail for historians like myself to follow. Thus, it took me over thirty years to reach the conclusion recorded in this book and its prequel. The results are based on numerous letters written during the time these events occurred, (one such letter was chased across three States!) and at later times when corresponding with me, giving me quotes from their ancestor's diaries and other papers. Such a history has never been recorded before and piecing everything together gave a very different perspective on the whole affair. Obviously, some of the language used represents the times of the events and does not reflect the attitudes of the author or the publishers, in modern times.

Introduction

A person once asked me, 'what good is history in today's world? It is a dead subject.' I bristled at this question, although I genially replied, 'You couldn't be more wrong. History is very much alive and by learning from the past we can build a better future.'

In my first book, *The Battle of the Little Big Horn: A New Appraisal*, I laid the foundations for rewriting history and for exposing the truth concerning the death of George Armstrong Custer at the Little Big Horn in June 1876.

This second book, *The Aftermath of the Battle of the Little Big Horn*, primarily concentrates on how the atrocious conspiracy was cleverly concealed to promote the lie the conspirators had created and nurtured for posterity.

Fortunately for us, history doesn't work like that. The truth surrounding any high profile event will force its way through the web of deceit against all odds to be recognised. Elizabeth Custer spent the whole of her life, as a widow, trying in vain to eradicate the awful term characterising her late husband as a 'glory hunter'. There was no way she could succeed, but she tried anyway. Libby Custer was up against ruthless and powerful men who would abuse their position and use all their powers to preserve their own integrity, especially at the expense of others, dead or alive. Still, she tried, touring all the states to promote a totally different picture of George that had been so skilfully painted. She attended meetings and wrote books detailing her life with him. For the serious historian, her efforts were not in vain. She has left a plethora of letters and documents that show a very different person from the officer who rode to his death along the banks of the Little Big Horn.

Major Marcus Reno, Custer's second in command, had also been tarnished with the label of disobeying orders, as Custer had, even though neither of them had done so. They had both followed their orders to the letter and had been made scapegoats for the disaster. There was one difference though, Reno was still alive and could fight back and fight back he did by requesting a court of inquiry to investigate his actions in the field that fateful day.

Here was another chance for the conspirators to interfere with military judicature and they did. The Reno Court of Inquiry (as it became known) was deftly manipulated from day one with useless witnesses being specially chosen to take the stand and pre–prepared questions set to obscure the outcome. It was a complete whitewash and everyone knew it, however Reno was eventually absolved of any blame.

Not so for George Armstrong Custer. His manufactured 'infamy' was to live on for decades, until now. Finally, the truth is in the open; it is nasty in nature, but then much of humankind is nasty and out on the plains nothing was taken for granted. People could lose themselves, murders could be buried deep, and nature was always harsh on the soul. In essence, the plains were unforgiving if you made a mistake. George Custer made that mistake. He trusted his superiors; a trust that resulted in his terrible untimely death at the hands of a people who had become the instruments of murder through no fault of their own.

So, how many readers still think that history is dull and useless? The Indian Wars was one of the most colourful events of the era. It was unique, but then all history is unique in its own way. I hope my work has made history come alive for my readers. Don't accept the traditional concepts in average history books. Look beyond the words and sentences. Chase the clues and discover what history is all about.

W.A. Wallace
May 2022

PART ONE

'We drink to the memory of the brave,
The faithful and the few:
Some lie far off beyond the wave,
Some sleep in Ireland too.
All are gone; but still live on
The flame of those who died;
All true men, like you, men,
Remember them with pride.'

John K. Ingram

Chapter 1

A Military Affair

A whole century had passed since the signing of the 'Declaration of Independence' on 4th July 1776 and a great deal had happened in those hundred years for a young America to emerge from its shell and take its rightful place in the world as a true Democratic nation. At least, that was the theory if not the practice, for the definition of the word 'democracy' is usually defined as:

> 'a government by the people, usually through elected representatives, giving equality of rights in society.'

True, representatives were elected, but not all of the people had the right to vote. Having abolished slavery with the 13th Amendment of the Constitution, the government followed through with the 14th Amendment of 1868 in which all African Americans were granted suffrage. Not surprisingly, there remained a clause in the 14th Amendment that excluded Indians or Native Americans from the right to vote. It would take another fifty-six years of political harassing before Indians would be granted citizenship.

In his first inaugural address of 1869, Ulysses S. Grant noted the inequality the Indians were subject to when he stated:

> 'The proper treatment of the original occupants of this land ... the Indians, is one deserving of careful study. I will favour any course toward them which tends to their civilization and ultimate citizenship.'

Yet Grant did not explain why Indians were excluded, nor did he do anything to rectify it. His second inaugural address of 1873 appears to reflect more on how the United States would be viewed by other nations when dealing with native Indians, for he stated:

> 'Our superiority of strength and advantages of civilisation should make us lenient toward the Indian …
>
> If the effort is made in good faith, we will stand better before the civilised nations of the earth and our own consciousness for having made it.'

It is a shameful fact that Grant did not pursue the policies he advocated, but then politics was and still is a war of words and Grant did not have the support of the military for his propositions. Physical engagements are military affairs and such problems are the responsibility of the army.

The early years of the autonomous nation were plagued with political difficulties, both internal and international. Having established a legitimate status, the United States of America found itself hemmed in on all frontiers by other countries' possessions. To the north, the British had established a firm foothold in Canada with a large portion of the boundary naturally controlled by the Great Lakes. The 'Revolutionary War' had been a costly venture for both sides, as wars generally are, and although the British were defeated, the American government neither had the inclination nor the means to incur another war on that front.

The Spanish had expanded their territories to include all the lands west of the Mississippi River and a long stretch across the southern extremes that encompassed the city of New Orleans and the State of Florida. Early pioneers had crossed the Appalachian Mountains to find a heavily wooded expanse, rich in game and extremely fertile. Initial contact with the Spanish colonists gave the impression that this land could either be purchased by diplomacy or taken by military force.

Daniel Boone had cut a trail towards the Ohio River that would become known as 'the Wilderness Road'. Others had moved north, but a large number of settlers traversed around the southern end of the Appalachians to establish communities in the 'Old Southwest'. It was an age of expansion, fraught with danger and excitement and yet, it seemed to lay the very foundations of the American frontier spirit. Whilst their government used diplomacy to acquire new territories, the intrepid settlers pushed further west, often causing clashes with the Spanish authorities and minor diplomatic problems, yet their thirst for expansion was insatiable.

The Louisiana Purchase of 1803 opened up huge areas of rich, fertile land and with the Mississippi no longer under Spanish control, the impatient settlers surged west. For those who survived the extreme hardships of a westward trek, the rewards were endless. But for those who fell by the wayside, too exhausted to push any further, the reward was one long struggle for survival, even death. The Indians had watched this expansion from the onset and on being displaced from their lands, violent clashes broke out; first with the Iroquois and Cherokee and then with the more deadly Comanche and Sioux. Pushed beyond the extremes, the Indians fought back and more and more frequently the horizon would be ablaze in the early hours of the morning as another settlement or lone ranch was razed to the ground. Aware of such dangers, settlers still continued their advance west and the further they travelled, the greater became their civilisation.

It was these innovative pathfinders, living on a razor's edge between life and death, who would eventually become the builders of modern America. Along those early trails, now widened by the rolling wheels of endless wagon trains, small townships appeared that grew larger in size and numbers. Frontier outposts sprang up to protect the civilians from Indian raids, although the military could never field enough men to solve the problem. Whilst some regarded the Indians as uncontrollable savages with the army powerless to curtail them, others merely regarded them as paupers who should be looked upon as a mild irritation and dealt with accordingly. Needless to say, the majority of the latter still resided in the east and had no idea of the hardships of frontier survival. In any event, the frontier, wherever it might be, was a lawless and untamed country that government officials would rather ignore in the vain hope it would sort itself out or move on.

By the 1870s, the seemingly endless roll of wagons had traversed the wide expanses bringing with them countless numbers of settlers, all eager to make a new life for themselves. Railroads quickly followed in their wake, taking advantage of this progressive movement to spread their arteries and deliver new ideas, technology, and trade to the towns. The slower riverboat was being edged into history by the faster wood –burning locomotives, thus by 1876 steamboats such as the 'Far West' had already reached the pinnacle of their careers when Marsh made his record- breaking journey in July. This was the age of progress and achievement, and it highlighted the irresistible drive into the future; a whole new way of life in a brave new world!

Thus, the American people had survived those tentative first hundred years of autonomy. They were tough, skilful, and resolute. Wars had been fought with battles lost and won, all of which had incurred a dreadful loss of life. However, lessons had been learned the hard way and progress was now forging ahead in leaps and bounds. It seems that there were no obstacles on the expanding frontier that could not be dealt with, or so they thought.

In the year of 1876, 'Independence Day' burst upon the scene with a magical kaleidoscope of fervent excitement and gay abandonment. There was no state, town, or humble abode that was not ablaze with the colours of red, white and blue, or with their national flag proudly fluttering in the breeze. For a whole two hours bands played non–stop; governors and mayors delivered rousing speeches to those who were sober enough to listen; whilst the populace engaged in eating, drinking, and dancing until they dropped, whatever their age. On the frontier, all hope of retaining any semblance of law and order was simply abandoned, but then, according to statistics, very few had any inclination of committing a felony that day. All thoughts on the current military operations against the Sioux and Cheyenne had been extinguished only to be rekindled with a vengeance some forty-eight hours later. Along the Yellowstone and upper Missouri rivers, word had inevitably reached the forts and outlying townships that Custer and his battalion had been wiped out by the hostiles, but it was generally dismissed as fanciful rumours and suppressed by the local dignitaries, who were not going to have their centennial celebrations marred by such malicious gossip.

For the survivors of the Seventh Cavalry there were no jubilant festivities that year. Camped on the Yellowstone, they were mentally and physically exhausted. The less seriously wounded had been left in the care of Paulding in his makeshift hospital and were well on the way to recovery, although mentally some would never recover from such a traumatic experience. In fact, just two weeks later, Captain Lewis Thompson, Second Cavalry, shot himself with his revolver. The official verdict of his suicide was attributed to his neuralgia and the fact that he could no longer endure his nervous disposition. However, troopers had their own thoughts concerning his death as Private Taylor wrote:

> '… It was believed by many and so stated in camp at the time, that the hardships of the campaign and the horrors of the Custer battlefield had, as it undoubtedly had done to others, unsettled his mind.'

There is little information regarding this episode of the campaign although medical reports state that overall, four other officers and over twenty enlisted men from both Terry's and Crook's columns, were presumed unfit for duty and sent home, several of whom were actually insane.

On the 4th July a petition was circulated amongst the enlisted men of the Seventh Cavalry. It was believed to have originated at Reno's headquarters, presumably to defend any legal action that could result from the battle, such as a court of inquiry or court martial, although there is no positive proof of this origin. In any event, it was passed through the ranks by the new chief trumpeter, Felix V. Vinatieri, and was eventually signed by 235 men, most of whom did so considering a refusal could offend the officers involved. Addressed to the President and the representatives of the United States, it began:

> 'We the enlisted men the survivors of the battle on the Heights of Little Horn River, on 25th and 26th of June 1876, of the 7th Regiment of Cavalry who subscribe our names to this petition, most earnestly solicit the President and Representatives of our Country, that the vacancies among the officers of our Regiment, made by the slaughter of our brave, heroic, now lamented Lieutenant Colonel George A. Custer, and the other noble dead Commissioned Officers of our Regiment who fell close to him on the bloody field, daring the savage demons to the last, be filled by the Officers of the Regiment only …'

The petition then continues to request that Major M. Reno should be promoted to lieutenant colonel, thus filling the position now vacated by Custer; and that the other vacancies to be filled by the remaining officers according to their seniority. It is obvious that the petition had been written by someone only partially versed in military rules or etiquette, for the document actually states that their request is 'contrary to the established rule.' Officers would, or should, have been aware that such promotions were generally made according to seniority of rank and service, not necessarily in the same regiment. The enlisted men would not have been aware of this. Nevertheless, it was not common practice for enlisted men to concern themselves with regimental policies and the actual identity of the author of the petition still remains a mystery. Finally, the petition details Reno's participation in the engagement and ends by stating that if Reno had not taken the defensive position on the bluff then no–one would be alive to tell the tale.

As the senior officer in the field for the Seventh, Reno would have known that such a defeat would call for a court of inquiry and that someone, probably himself, would end up being the scapegoat at a court martial. He also knew that at the end of the day he would have to answer for his conduct during the fight. If Reno did not write the petition, he must have been aware of its existence and would have realised that it could be useful if needed for his defence. As Sergeant George McDermott of Company A, remarked at the time,

> "It was damned humbug, but what's the odds?"

Considering the number of enlisted men who signed the petition represented approximately 80 % of the survivors of the Seventh, it appears to be pretty good odds at the end of the day!

All soldiers know that what happens in the military stays in the military, so the question is why was the petition sent to the President and not through Sheridan first? It was inevitable that the petition would never reach Grant anyway. However, it did journey through the labyrinth of official military channels until it reached Sherman, who was clearly irritated on having received it. His reply dated 5th August, was noticeably curt:

> 'The judicious and skilful conduct of Major Reno and Captain Benteen is appreciated, but the promotions caused by General Custer's death have been made by the President and confirmed by the Senate; therefore, this petition cannot be granted.
>
> … commissions can only be granted by the President on the advice and consent of the Senate, and except in original vacancies, promotion in a regiment is generally, if not always, made on the rule of seniority.'

However, Sherman's reply is extremely interesting for it clearly states that the promotions to fill Custer's vacancy had already been approved by Grant. Promotion within the military was an extremely slow process at this time, especially on the frontier where officers could be completely forgotten and remain at the lower echelon for ten years or more. Officers applying for a promotional post would have to pass a selection committee before coming under the scrutiny of the Senate and only then would their recommendations be passed to the President. With an election year about to start, officer promotions would not necessarily have been a priority within government circles and Grant's administration was still reeling from the recent scandals that had become public knowledge. Thus, what was normally a lengthy and time-consuming process, would have taken longer to become effective. The time factor here is also worthy of note. The petition was signed on the 4 July and it would have reached Washington shortly after the first reports had been received from Terry via Sheridan, which was the 6th July. Assuming the petition did not reach Sherman until the 12th July at the outset, that would give approximately two weeks to select and replace around eleven officers, have the selection approved by the president and the chosen officer duly notified. Official papers show that these officers were assigned their new posts in the Seventh Cavalry during July, before Sherman's reply to the petition on the 5th August and before his request for additional troops on the 11th August. Had these officers already been chosen by Sheridan and Sherman when they formulated their diabolical plan; the removal of Custer to protect the reputation of Grant? It certainly appears to be the case, even though the evidence is purely circumstantial. There is no other explanation.

The commanding officer of the Seventh Cavalry was Colonel Samuel D. Sturgis, whose son, Lieutenant James G. Sturgis, had been killed at the Little Big Horn. A graduate of West Point, Samuel Sturgis does not appear to have had a very distinguished career. During the Mexican War he was captured whilst making a reconnaissance near Buena Vista and his service during the Civil War gives the impression that he had taken part in more Union defeats than victories. Indeed, a closer look at his service record shows that he appeared to favour departmental posts rather than actual engagements with the enemy and although he took command of the Seventh on 6th May 1869, he was hardly ever present with the regiment. Sturgis seemed to prefer spending most of his time on detached service, leaving George Custer as the acting commanding officer in his absence. In fact, as the official commanding officer, Sturgis managed to evade his duties for over six years, which is some feat! He was on detached duty in St. Louis when the Seventh took to the field in 1876, the reasons for which had never been satisfactorily explained.

The officer chosen to replace Custer was Major (Brevet Colonel) Elmer Otis, who, on acceptance of the position, was promoted to lieutenant colonel. Otis had graduated from West Point in 1853, the same year that Phil Sheridan had, so it can be assumed that they at least knew each other. According to official records, Otis served in the 1st Cavalry as a second lieutenant at the same time that Sturgis was serving as a captain in the regiment. Thus, it can be safely assumed that Otis and Sturgis knew each other. Given his first lieutenancy in 1856, Otis remained with the Second until the re-organisations in 1861, when his regiment became the Fourth Cavalry and he was promoted to captain. On 15th February 1862, Otis applied for a colonelcy in the Ohio Volunteers and his application included recommendations from persons of high rank who had known him for years. Were these people Sturgis and Sheridan? He was refused the position, although by the end of the Civil War he had attained the rank of major, still serving in the Fourth Cavalry. Otis retained this rank until his promotion to lieutenant colonel of the Seventh Cavalry in 1876.

Like Sturgis, his military career is not very impressive. Although he had seen combat service on the Indian frontier, his only claim to fame was the council he held with Captain Jack on 13th April 1872, during the Modoc War and that did not achieve anything either. Thus, in Otis, Sheridan had the perfect replacement for Custer and as he was also known to Sturgis, there would be no disagreement there. Official records state that Otis became lieutenant colonel of the Seventh Cavalry on 25th June 1876 the very day of Custer's death! With Sturgis on detached service, away from his regiment in the field, Sheridan appears to have been fairly certain that Custer would be killed and if that is the case, then the recommendation of the appointment of Otis from Sherman so early is proof that Sherman knew of Sheridan's plan and approved it.

With so many vacancies caused by the deaths of so many officers, it is not surprising that the Seventh Cavalry underwent a re-organisation during July. What is surprising is that very few promotions occurred within the regiment itself and none involving senior officers. Only three existing second lieutenants, Winfield S. Edgerly, George D. Wallace and Charles A. Varnum were promoted to first lieutenants to fill the vacancies left by officers who had either been killed or re-organised within the regiment. This left a large number of second lieutenant positions that were filled from other cavalry regiments, in fact a total of twelve and all the appointments had been made during July!

Whilst the petition was being circulated on the 4th July, Captain Benteen wrote a report concerning the operations of his battalion and submitted it through the regimental adjutant, Lieutenant Wallace, to Major Reno. Benteen clearly states that he deployed his troops in accordance with verbal instructions he had received from Reno and detailed his movements until the uniting with Reno on the bluff. However, upon receipt of the urgent message delivered by Trumpeter Martin, he does not explain why he did not fulfil the request. He duly notes his observations of the repulse of Reno's charge:

> '... brought me in sight of the stream and plain in which were some of our dismounted men fighting and Indians charging and recharging them in great numbers. The plain seemed to be alive

> with them. I then noticed our men in large numbers running for the bluffs on the right bank of the stream. I concluded at once that those had been repulsed, and was of the opinion that if I crossed the ford with my battalion, that I should have had it treated in like manner; for from long experience with cavalry, I judged there were 900 veteran Indians right there at that time, against which the large element of recruits in my battalion would stand no earthly chance as mounted men.'

Benteen is very careful in his choice of words, although at the Reno Court of Inquiry three years later, he elucidated further:

> 'There I saw an engagement going on and supposed it was the whole regiment …
>
> I thought the whole command was thrashed …
>
> Then I saw the men who were up on the bluff and I immediately went there and was met by Major Reno.'

However, it must be borne in mind that Benteen's report and his statement at the inquiry would have been influenced by additional facts concerning the battle that he would not have been aware of at the time as he was not an actual participant. Benteen never disclosed his reasons for not responding to Custer's urgent messages, not once but twice! And his intense dislike for the lieutenant colonel was common knowledge throughout the regiment, indeed he firmly believed that Custer was responsible for the death of Major Elliott at the Battle of the Washita and this had led to clashes between the two men on more than one occasion. Was this vehement dislike that had burnt inside him for so many years enough for him to deliberately kill his commanding officer and his men and did it influence his decision not to go to Custer's aid with the result that he was possibly instrumental in the disaster? We will never know. What is known is that Benteen received information from his cousin prior to the expedition. What this information was, we do not know, but did this information influence his decision not to go to Custer's aid? Benteen's letters to his wife whilst on campaign are extremely interesting and give tantalising hints that he knew much more of the facts surrounding the battle than he was prepared to divulge. In a letter written on 2nd July 1876 at the confluence of the Big Horn with the Yellowstone, Benteen is relating his experiences and when writing of the numbers of hostile Indians they encountered, he says:

> 'There were 5,000 of them - so General Sheridan telegraphs General Terry.'

Five thousand was a far cry from the 1500 that the Commissioner of Indian Affairs had advised they would probably encounter. As Sheridan was the first senior military commander to be informed of the disaster, and only just, how could he respond to Terry with a more accurate figure so quickly? Unless he already knew and had not let it be known. Whatever his reasons may be, Reno was certainly glad that Benteen had made the decision to remain with him on the bluff, for in his official report the major wrote:

> 'During my fight with the Indians I had the heartiest support from the officers and men, but the conspicuous service of Bvt. Col. F.W. Benteen, I desire to call attention to especially; for if ever a soldier deserved recognition by his government for distinguished service, he certainly did.'

Major Marcus Reno wrote his official report on the 5th July and duly submitted it, together with Benteen's report, to General Terry through the general's adjutant, Captain E.W. Smith. It may be safely assumed that Reno's report actually went through Smith's office, as the captain was on the 'Far West' at the time, on his way to report to General Sheridan. Reno's report is quite lengthy and gives full details of actions against the hostiles involving his battalion. It makes very interesting reading, for together with Terry's final orders, it actually absolves Custer of any blame for the debacle that followed. Reno clearly states that by the early hours of the morning on the 25th June:

> '... About 8 a.m. his command was in the valley of one of the branches of the Little Big Horn; by this time Indians had been seen and it was certain that we could not surprise them and it was determined to move at once to the attack.'

This complies with Terry's orders giving Custer 'sufficient reason'. The report then details his conversation with Lieutenant Cooke, who verbally relayed Custer's orders:

> '... to move forward at as rapid a gait as prudent and to charge afterwards and that the whole outfit would support me.'

Assured of Custer's support, Reno then detailed his fight in the valley; the retreat to the bluffs; and the defensive position he held until relieved by Terry and Gibbon. The report ends with details of those killed and wounded within the regiment. Surprisingly, Reno concludes his analysis of Custer's decision to divide the regiment as being tactically correct, for he writes:

> 'I think had the regiment gone in a body, and from the woods from which I fought advanced upon the village, it's destruction was certain.'

Over the years since the battle, both Custer and Reno have been held accountable for the disaster and this had been a gross miscarriage of justice. Both men were victims of circumstance. Custer had been deliberately placed in a situation from which he found it impossible to extricate himself. Reno followed his orders and when he discovered he was no longer able to do so, he executed a tactical withdrawal to a position from where his troops could defend themselves and await the promised support from Custer that never came. Unfortunately for Reno, others did not view his situation in the same light and he was openly accused of 'cowardice in the face of the enemy' and of leaving Custer to his fate. Surviving officers, in both Reno's and Benteen's battalions, later testified when questioned that they observed no evidence of cowardice on the part of Reno, indeed, Benteen actually stated that Reno's conduct was good and that his actions were correct. At the court of inquiry, Lieutenant Wallace stated that:

> 'At no time did I observe any failure upon Major Reno's part to do the duty expected and required of a commanding officer.'

If this was the general consensus, then where did the accusations that Reno was a coward and abandoned Custer originate? The answer, for the most part, can be found in Captain Edward Godfrey, officer commanding Company K in Benteen's battalion. Throughout his military career, Godfrey was a prolific writer, particularly on the Indian Wars, and the Godfrey family papers contain far more material on his histories than on his own experiences as a soldier. It appears that Godfrey had very little regard for Reno as an officer and the disaster at the Little Big Horn gave him an opportunity to publicly cast doubts on the major's competence. Given that Godfrey did not actually witness Reno's attack on the Indian village, his vehement condemnation of

Reno must have been based on hearsay, camp rumours, and his own biased opinion. Benteen, who had little time for Godfrey, or anyone else for that matter, could see that he was using the battle and Custer's name to increase his finances and social standing, whether he was writing the truth or not. In fact, over the following years Benteen was to write numerous letters himself to Theodore Goldin, a former private in Company A and a Medal of Honour winner during the battle, concerning the conduct of the officers of the regiment and the campaign of 1876, amongst other things. However, for the public to have a hero, they must also be given a scapegoat. Godfrey's articles gave them a hero in Custer and a villain in Reno, which the public believed unconditionally and clamoured for more. At the court of inquiry, Godfrey endorsed his fellow officers when they stated that Reno had shown no fear or cowardice during the battle, yet at the same time he wrote:

> 'At no time during the battle was his conduct such as to inspire confidence or respect.'

In later years he went even further, for when asked for the reasons he considered were contributory to Custer's defeat, he firmly replied that 'Reno's panic from the valley' was the major factor. If numerous military personnel were not impressed, others were, including Elizabeth Custer, who would do anything to preserve the name of her late husband, and Frederick Whittaker, who would produce an idealised biography of Custer and ultimately would be instrumental in forcing the military to convene an inquiry. Sheridan and Sherman must have been delighted at this pressurised condemnation of Reno and, in allowing Reno to be publicly ostracised for the disaster, they had the perfect cover for their conspiratorial actions and; the circumstantial evidence does lead to this conclusion. Their combined actions may have preserved the president's reputation from being tarnished any further but they had also condemned over 200 innocent soldiers to a gruesome death and Grant remained oblivious of his friend's role in the drama until his death in 1885, for he wrote:

> 'I regard Custer's massacre as an unnecessary sacrifice of troops brought on by Custer himself.'

Did Grant know of the conspiracy between Sheridan and Sherman? His remark is certainly ambiguous. If he did know he said nothing, preferring to remain apart from such murderous deeds.

THE AFTERMATH OF THE BATTLE OF LITTLE BIG HORN

During the early hours of the 6th July, officers at Fort Lincoln were aroused and instructed to report to headquarters, where they were duly informed of the fate concerning Custer and his men. It has been stated in some accounts that the news of the battle reached the fort a week before the 'Far West' brought the official report. Apparently, two Crow scouts, Horned Toad and Speckled Cock, both having recently been employed as guides for Gibbon's column, arrived at Fort Rice, in Montana, within days of the fight and excitedly related the news of Custer's death. To embellish their story they informed a captive audience that Custer had shot himself and it is their lies that form the origin of the myth that Custer committed suicide. The two Crows then rode to Fort Lincoln where they relayed their tale again, this time in the presence of Elizabeth Custer and other wives, who upon hearing the dreadful news shrieked and ran from the room. It has also been claimed that military authorities suppressed this incident. There are no such records to confirm or denounce the event and as such, there is no evidence to corroborate any of these incidents. However, the fact that these two Indians were scouts in Gibbon's command and turned up at the two forts, suggests that the incidents could possibly be true. The response to their story by Elizabeth Custer, and the other wives, does seem improbable as rumours of one kind or another, circulated by the Indians to instil fear, were common occurrences on the frontier and it is doubtful if officers' wives would believe such stories or display such behaviour.

In any event, just before sunrise on 6th July, a delegation consisting of Captain W. McCaskey, Lieutenant C. Gurley, Doctor J. Middleton and two medical assistants arrived at the Custer quarters. Lieutenant Gurley, 6th Infantry, describes the scene:

> 'I went to the rear of the Custer house, woke up Maria, Mrs Custer's housemaid and requested her to rap on Mrs Custer's door, and to say to her that she and Mrs Calhoun and Miss Reed were wanted in the parlour. But Mrs Custer had been awakened by the footsteps in the hall. She called me by name and asked me the cause of my early visit …'

With the ladies assembled in the parlour, the calamity at the Little Big Horn was tactfully relayed. The grief these women must have felt is indescribable, yet Elizabeth Custer dutifully accompanied the men to the quarters of the other widows.

Apart from the official report on the battle, Elizabeth Custer received no letter from Sherman or the War Department and nothing from President Grant either. However, she did receive a government pension of $50 per month and a cheque for $4,750 from the New York Life Insurance Company. George Custer's insurance policy, number 106.707, was written on the 4th June 1874, naming his wife as the sole beneficiary and was for $5,000. The premium was apparently $25.56 per thousand and it carried an extra premium of five per cent for 'war risk', which if not paid by the time of Custer's death would have been deducted from the payment.

Other officers of the Seventh Cavalry also provided for their next of kin through insurance policies with the New York Life Insurance Company: Lieutenant James Calhoun's policy, written on the 1st June 1874, was also for $5,000 and named his wife, Margaret, as the beneficiary. Likewise, the policy of Captain George Yates, written on the 19th July 1874, was for $5,000 and payable to his wife. However, it appears that the policies of Captain Myles Keogh and Lieutenant John Crittenden may have carried a double indemnity clause, for their beneficiaries received $10,000. Keogh's policy was written on the 13th June 1873 and rumours abounded that he had named himself as the beneficiary. Of course that was not true. He actually named his sister, who lived in Ireland, who received $9,000 and his best friend, Lieutenant Henry Nowland who received $1,000. Crittenden's policy was written on the 12th May 1876, naming his mother as the sole beneficiary. All of the policies were written by I.F.A. Studdart of St. Paul, Minnesota, who was an agent for the New York Life Insurance Company, with his agency covering the northern, central western states. If he was astute enough to encompass the majority of the forts in his area, Studdart must have earned a very pleasant income from the policies he sold to the officers alone. All of the policies mentioned here were paid out by the company, who must have at some time considered army officers serving on the frontier a doubtful insurance risk!

Terry had still received no word from Crook and he had no idea of the whereabouts of Crook's forces. Then on the 7th July, a party of Crow scouts arrived at Terry's camp carrying dispatches from Crook, informing Terry of his fight on the Rosebud of the 17th June. The following day, Terry sent a telegram to his headquarters in St. Paul, requesting that it be forwarded to Sherman. The telegram makes no mention of having received word from Crook and appears to be a reiteration of his reports to Sheridan, stating Custer's defeat and listing those known to have been killed, with a request that their families be duly notified. On the 9th July Terry wrote to Crook, also informing him of Custer's defeat and of Gibbon's movements. He also informed Crook that the commands under himself and Gibbon, including the survivors of the Seventh Cavalry, were at present on the Yellowstone and discloses his own fears on the campaign when he writes:

> 'The great and, to me, wholly unexpected strength which the Indians have developed seem to me to make it important and indeed necessary that we should unite to at least act in close co-operation. In my ignorance of your present position and of the position of the Indians, I am unable to propose a plan for this, but if you will devise one and communicate it to me, I will follow it.
>
> … I hope it is unnecessary for me to say that should our forces unite, even in my own Department, I shall assume nothing by reason of my seniority but shall be prepared to co-operate with you in the most cordial and hearty manner, leaving you entirely free to pursue your own course.'

Clearly Terry would welcome the additional insurance of Crook's forces and he would not be disappointed if Crook assumed overall command. In fact, it appears that Terry is requesting Crook to do just that. It is also possible that Terry has realised the full implications behind the orders he had received from Sheridan, for he is now very reluctant to resume operations against the hostiles and he remained on the Yellowstone until the 28th July, when he moved camp to the mouth of the Rosebud.

Terry's dispatch was carried to Crook by three privates of Company E, 7th Infantry: James Bell, William Evans, and Benjamin Stewart. Gibbon later described the volunteers:

> 'Evans and Stewart were both tall, gaunt, lank specimens of humanity, and looked as if a hard days ride would use them up completely. Bell was short, and more stoutly made. All of them appeared to be very quiet men, did not light up at all in conversation, and exhibited no enthusiasm whatsoever.'

Considering they were going to ride south to find Crook, through country crawling with hostiles, it is hardly surprising they were not enthusiastic. Nonetheless, the couriers reached Cook's camp on 12th July, totally exhausted from their journey. All three men were awarded the Congressional Medal of Honour for their bravery:

> 'Carried dispatches to General Crook through country occupied by Sioux, at imminent risk of life.

Crook had remained in his camp on Goose Creek since his defeat at the Battle of the Rosebud on 19th June, much to the chagrin of many of his command and thus providing his critics with the fuel of their condemnation. On 30th June the 'Helena Daily Independent' printed a severe critical report of the battle, written by an unknown correspondent stationed at Fort Laramie:

> 'The officers of the post speak in terms of unmeasured condemnation of Gen. Crook's behaviour and denounce his retreat in the face of the savage enemy as cowardly. It is also reported that the Crows have refused to stay with Crook any longer…
>
> … And as the details of the affair became known, it is looked upon as humiliating and disgraceful to the last degree.'

Crook, however, appears to be unmoved by the determined newspaper coverage. As far as he was concerned he had obeyed his orders and when he read Terry's dispatch informing him of Custer's defeat, he gave no hint of his feelings regarding the matter. Captain Anson Mills, of the 3rd Cavalry, later described Crook as:

> '… A cold, grey–eyed and somewhat cold–bloodied warrior…'

During the Civil War, Crook had got into difficulties and Custer had gone to his aid, saving him from certain defeat. Crook had deeply resented Custer's action and never forgave him for it.

In his camp, Crook and his forces had not been totally devoid of any further action, having endured a number of irritating raids by Sioux warriors over the weeks they remained there. Sergeant George Howard, of Company E, Second Cavalry, wrote in his diary for the 10th July:

> 'We had quite a battle last night, making ten so far this summer. The Indians accomplished nothing but firing the prairie which caused us some trouble.'

It is worth noting that between them, Crook and Terry had approximately 2,000 troops under their command, yet neither of them resumed the campaign without receiving substantial re-enforcements. A far cry from their confident prediction earlier that year, that they could easily whip the hostiles into submission and put them all on the reservations to contain them! Or was it all part of the plan?

Nevertheless, on 13th July Crook received his re-enforcements and much needed supplies from Fort Fetterman. Included in the increment were ten companies of the 5th Cavalry under Colonel Wesley Merritt, although these troops did not actually reach Crook until 3rd August. Thus, when all his troops were assembled and ready to march, Crook had over 2,000 troops under his command: twenty-five companies of cavalry from the 2nd, 3rd and 5th Regiments under Colonel Merritt and ten infantry companies of the 4th, 9th and 14th Regiments commanded by Major Alexander Chambers. In addition, Crook had the services of over 200 Shoshone warriors under Chief Washakie and an enormous pack train that carried fifteen days' supply of rations. By 3rd August Crook was ready to march north and follow the Rosebud, where he hoped to find Terry and further supplies. It could also be assumed that Crook had endured enough humiliation to make him resume the campaign or, alternatively, he had executed his original orders successfully and had received new information from Sheridan. Whatever the reason, Crook was on the move again, giving his command some hope of redemption for their commander's spurious behaviour.

Elsewhere, Custer's defeat had caused a chain reaction that could only spell disaster for the victorious Indians. Sherman allowed his military commanders to blame the Bureau of Indian Affairs for supplying inaccurate, or even false, information and for allowing countless numbers of warriors to slip away from the agencies to join the hostile bands. Naturally, the Bureau retaliated and accused the army of incompetence, although their own ability was seriously in question. Letters from army officers, stationed near the reservations did not help to clarify the situation, even though they were probably written with the best of intentions. Sheridan received one such letter, dated 14th July, from Captain J.S. Poland, 6th Infantry stationed at the Standing Rock Agency in Dakota. Poland states that there are huge discrepancies between the reports of the Indian agents and the true facts, as he perceives them. He cites the case of the previous agent, Edmund Palmer, who reported that he had 6,440 Indians on the reservation for 1874, although Poland was not aware of any more than 4,500 for the same year. Poland then adds that the subsequent agent, John Burke, has continued this practice, as Burke has falsely reported that he has over 7,000 Indians in his charge. Obviously, this suggests that the agents are operating a scam using the rations and Poland does not mince words in making that understood, thus he conducted an investigation himself:

> 'I determined to count the lodges here and I now report the actual number within a radius of several miles (kilometres). There are less than 300. Two hundred and ninety–six, to which may be added perhaps fifty more which are legitimately engaged in hunting game …
>
> There are not here now 1500 Indians.'

Poland asserts that there have been never more than forty–five hundred Indians at the agency and that the agent's reports to the contrary were,

> '… Made knowingly and with the fraudulent intent … of procuring and profiteering by the secret and unauthorised sale of supplies, rations and annuities …'

Continuing a relentless bombardment of accusations, Poland concludes that the Indians who abandon reservation life to join the hostile camps were forced to do so or their families would face starvation. He actually calculates the numbers of Indians known to have left the agencies and claims that Sitting Bull has probably between five and six thousand warriors at his disposal. The resolute captain was not far from the truth!

Sheridan must have received numerous letters such as this, as indeed other departmental commanders did. However, Poland's letter, in particular, has the appearance of a double–edged sword. Whilst it clearly accuses the Indian agents of falsifying their reports, thus putting the blame on the Bureau of Indian Affairs, it also provides evidence to support Custer's accusations against Belknap (amongst others), incurring the displeasure of the president. Sheridan and Sherman would welcome the former, but would find the latter awkward, perhaps even a threat. Sheridan did not forward Poland's letter to Sherman for almost a month, allowing the bureaucrats in Washington to fight amongst themselves. On 22nd July the Senate reached a decision and Sherman was given the authority for the military to assume complete control over the reservations situated in Sioux country and to treat all residents as prisoners of war. Officials in the Bureau of Indian Affairs were devastated. Not only was this a direct insult against their integrity but it also meant the loss of authority over their agents in the field at a time when diplomatic relations with their charges was imperative.

As if to endorse the Senate's decision, Sheridan received another letter from Captain Poland two days later. In his report, Poland states that his information was obtained from seven Sioux Indians who were known to have participated in the fight at the Little Big Horn. He also accuses the agent of suppressing reports concerning the return of hostile warriors and of instructing the warriors not to circulate their stories of the event. As this report is probably the first recorded version of the battle from the Indian's perspective, the pertaining portion of the report is included in its entirety:

> 'The hostiles were celebrating their greatest of religious festivals –the Sun Dance–when runners brought news of the approach of cavalry. The dance was suspended and a general rush (mistaken by Custer perhaps, for a retreat) for horses, equipment and arms followed. Major Reno first attacked the village at the south end and across the Little Big Horn. Their narrative of Reno's operations coincides with the published accounts; how he was quickly confronted, surrounded; how he dismounted, rallied in the timber, remounted and cut his way back over the ford and up the bluffs with considerable loss; and the continuation of the fight for some little time, when runners arrived from the north end of the village, or camp, with the news that the cavalry had attacked the north end of the same—three or four miles [four to six kilometres] distant.
>
> The Indians about Reno had not before this the slightest intimation of fighting at any other point. A force large enough to prevent Reno from assuming the offensive was left and the surplus available force flew to the other end of the camp, where, finding the Indians there successfully driving Custer before them, instead of uniting with them, they separated into two parties and moved around the flanks of his cavalry.
>
> They report that he crossed the river, but only succeeded in reaching the edge of the Indian camp. After he was driven to the bluffs the fight lasted perhaps an hour. Indians have no hours of the day, and the time cannot be given approximately.
>
> They report that a small number of cavalry broke through the line of Indians in their rear and escaped, but

> was overtaken, within a distance of five or six miles [eight or nine kilometres], and killed. I infer from this that this body of retreating cavalry was probably led by the missing officers, and that they tried to escape only after Custer fell. The last man that was killed, was killed by two sons of a Santee Indian, 'Red-Top', who was a leader in the Minnesota Massacre of '62 and '63.
>
> After the battle the squaws entered the field to plunder and mutilate the dead. A general rejoicing was indulged in, and a distribution of arms and ammunition hurriedly made.
>
> Then the attack on Major Reno was vigorously renewed. Up to this attack, the Indians had lost comparatively few men, but now, they say, their most serious loss took place. They give no idea of numbers, but say there were a great many. Sitting Bull was neither killed nor personally engaged in the fight. He remained in the council tent directing operations.'

Poland then describes the principal leaders in the fight and the story of Kill Eagle, Chief of the Blackfoot. He then continues:

> 'The Indians were not all engaged at any one time; heavy reserves were held to repair losses and renew attacks successively. The fight continued until the third day when runners kept purposely on the lookout, hurried into the camp and reported a great body of troops (General Terry's column) advancing up the river.'

He then details the retreat of the hostiles and reports that the returning Indians will be trying to cajole the remaining reservation Indians into joining forces with the hostiles.

Poland's report is interesting for it confirms Reno's account and states that Custer was not the last man to fall. It contains so much valuable information and crushes the myth that gave rise to so many paintings of the fight. Had Poland's letters not been suppressed, Custer's legend could have been portrayed more accurately. The report also gave the army a rough position of the area where the hostiles could be found. Yet this was ignored and the army spent months fruitlessly trying to locate the elusive hostiles. Clearly Sheridan was alarmed by Poland's perseverance. On 11th August he forwarded Poland's original report, together with an endorsement of his own. Whilst admitting that Poland could possibly be correct, Sheridan concluded that the captain's personal bitterness of Indian agents rendered his report too doubtful to act upon. Sheridan resolved the problem by having Poland replaced by Lieutenant Colonel Carlin, although there is no evidence to throw any light on the fate of Poland. Obviously Poland was becoming a nuisance so Sheridan had him removed. The general also states that agent Burke will also be removed from his post. Sherman dutifully endorsed Sheridan's comments and forwarded the papers to the secretary of war. Poland's second report, which contained so much vital information to the campaign and future enquiries, was not referred to again. Captain Poland learned the hard way that field officers do not upset the plans laid by superior commanders, for he was not heard of again either.

By 11th August, Sherman had requested Congress to authorise an increase of at least 2,500 new recruits to swell the ranks of the cavalry regiments in the field. His request granted, a rapid military build-up began and throughout the early autumn the increases were very notable. The 2nd Cavalry was increased to 966 enlisted men; the 3rd Cavalry enlarged to 1,022 enlisted men; and the 5th Cavalry was expanded to 1,073 enlisted men. But it was the 7th Cavalry who received the largest number, 500 recruits from Jefferson Barracks brought its compliment to a total of 1,205 enlisted men. However, the increments within the cavalry regiments were so rapid that many of the new recruits could not even ride a horse, much less fire a weapon or fight Indians! But the cry throughout the country was "avenge Custer!" and so, men of all professions and nationalities rushed to the ranks. To Sherman such details were mere trivialities. He now had full control of the reservations and he had the forces to police them. The issue concerning the Indians, whether friendly or hostile, had become a military affair.

In the meantime, Terry had moved his forces on 27th July to a new location at the mouth of the Rosebud, where he set up a new supply camp and awaited the arrival of re-enforcements. The couriers he had sent to Crook had returned on 25th July bearing dispatches from the general and Terry knew what Crook's intentions were. Gibbon later wrote;

> 'The news they brought decided the plan of our future operations, and two days after their return we commenced the march to the mouth of the Rosebud, where for the present was to be our depot of supplies.'

In actual fact, Terry had no option but to move the supply camp. The Big Horn and the upper reaches of the Yellowstone were becoming shallower as the dry season took on a firm grip, thus making it ever more hazardous for the river steamers to continue to forward supplies. Knowing that Crook was following the Rosebud, Terry had made his camp where the river joined the Yellowstone and was thus still accessible to the steamers and regular supplies. Both commanders were aware that the hostile Indians were still within the vicinity and they moved their troops cautiously through the area. In fact, the hostiles had camped, at one point, directly between the two forces and had they the inclination they could have annihilated either of these commands on separate occasions. Fortunately for Terry and Crook, the Indians did not even consider the possibility. They were too busy with more important matters, oblivious to the fact that the military had declared war on all Indians, a move that was to signify the end for these proud masters of the Prairies.

Chapter 2

In Pursuit of Dreams

Any study of the Indian Wars will reveal that the energetic expansion of settlers into the untamed regions of the western frontier included no provision for the native Indians who were already occupying the area. That is an established fact. They were a nuisance, an irritation which would inhibit progress. Cries of the Indian existence and their desperate plight were but mere whispers quietly floating on the breeze through the corridors of power, where greedy politicians turned a deaf ear and grabbed all the chances they could to make a profit out of the appalling situation. The Sioux and Cheyenne uprising of 1876 was a last tragic attempt to open the doors the government had so firmly locked against them and when the doors did finally swing open, what issued forth was not quite what the Indians had hoped for or even expected. Instead of a re-evaluation of their deplorable treatment, columns of soldiers poured forth whose sole intent was to crush any resistance and herd them on to reservations like cattle.

General Sherman had never hidden his intense dislike for the plains Indians, or any other Indians for that matter. As early as 1868 he had stated:

> 'We have now selected and provided reservations…
>
> All who cling to their old hunting grounds are hostile and will remain so till killed off.'

To his brother John, he wrote:

> 'The more we can kill this year, the less will have to be killed the next year.'

With such homicidal views it is easy to see how Sheridan's plan regarding Custer materialised so quickly and Sherman was not alone in his views. The hostiles had inadvertently provided the place and the means, although the likes of Sitting Bull and Crazy Horse would never know they were the main players in such a deadly game.

On 22nd July the army were given control of all the Indian reservations across the frontier. For the military serving in these areas, it added even more pressure to their responsibilities and stretched their resources to the limit. For the Indians, however, this was a major blow, especially for the agency Indians who had remained on the reservations and had accepted all the degradations that life afforded them. They had had every opportunity to join the hostile bands but had chosen not to, even though the temptation to do so must have been overwhelming. It was the agency Indians who would be the first to feel the iron hand of the soldiers, many of whom still sought to avenge Custer's death. Stripped of their integrity and rounded up like lambs for the slaughter, the agency Indians were quickly placed under armed guards and watched every hour of the day. But there were still questions that remained unanswered concerning the Black Hills. Those sacred hills that lured so may prospectors to their lush slopes.

In late August another commission was formed to approach the Indians in an effort to purchase the Black Hills. The fact is, Grant's government had already decided on their devious methods of procuring this land the previous year and it was not by treaty. In his State of the Union Address, given on 7th December 1875, Grant clearly defines their position concerning these mineral rich hills:

> 'The discovery of gold in the Black Hills, a portion of the Sioux Reservation, has had the effect to induce a large emigration of miners to that point. Thus, for the effort to protect the treaty rights of the Indians to that section has been successful, but the next year will certainly witness a large increase of such emigration. The negotiations for relinquishment of the gold fields having failed, it will be necessary for Congress to adopt some measures to relieve the embarrassment growing out of the causes named. The secretary of the interior suggests that the supplies now appropriated for the sustenance of that people, being no longer obligatory under the treaty of 1868, but simply a gratuity, may be issued or withheld at his discretion.'

Grant does not explain why the appropriations are no longer obligatory under the terms of the treaty and he also fails to explain why the secretary of the interior has taken it upon himself to make such changes. In any event, these changes came into force when, on 15th August 1876, Congress declared that all Indians were to give up their rights to all land within the regions of the Black Hills and Powder River once and for all or their appropriations would cease. The commission who were now trying to secure the Black Hills would have been fully aware of this decree.

The commission was comprised of Newton Edmunds, an ex – politician; Bishop Whipple; Doctor Boules; Doctor Daniel; Judge Gaylord; Colonel George Manypenny, a former Commissioner of Indian Affairs; and Colonel Boone, a grandson of the legendary Daniel Boone. Their initial attempts to draw the Indians to a council were complete failures, primarily due to the fact that many of the Indians who were now residing on the reservations had previously taken part in the Battle of the Little Big Horn and were reluctant to talk about another treaty. Eventually, around the middle of September, the commission entered into their negotiations with the Indians. Chiefs representing the Sioux, the Northern Cheyenne, and the Arapaho all listened as the commissioners made their offer for the Black Hills. For ten days they sat in silence, offering no gesture of dissent or approval, but standing their ground: the Black Hills were not for sale. Finally, the commission grew impatient and invoked the Congressional decree: either sell or starve. Not wanting to witness the slow death of their people by starvation, the Indian representatives capitulated.

The following day the commission presented the Indians with the treaty for them to acknowledge, a treaty that had been prepared in advance and one that was not open to negotiation. The principal provisions of the treaty stipulated that the Indians would relinquish their rights to the Black Hills and all other Indian lands west of the 103 meridian and their unceded territories in the north, as specified in the 1868 treaty, and in exchange they would be given subsistence rations as long as they would be needed for the Indians' survival. In fact, the treaty of 1868 was virtually ripped apart as though it did not exist. That treaty had contained the clause that if any Indian land that had been ceded to them were offered for sale, three-fourths of all adult male Indians would have to agree to the transaction. The 1876 commission visited the chiefs of the tribes individually and obtained only their marks to the treaty, a percentage of approximately ten per cent of the male population. Violation upon violation had occurred, but the commissioners were smug in the knowledge that they had successfully secured the Black Hills, although they were never purchased as the Indians refused to sell.

Theft, blackmail, murder, and violation of treaties were nothing new to the Indians. As early as 1786, the noted politician Benjamin Franklin wrote to a French friend:

> '... Almost every war between the Indians and the whites has been occasioned by some injustice of the latter towards the former.'

Disarmed and without horses, the agency Indians had no alternative but to accept the terms. However, the interpretation of the treaty is open to further questioning concerning the hostile Indians who later returned to the reservation to discover they had not been consulted on the matter. In July 1918, Magpie, a Cheyenne of 67 years old, made a statement to the Commissioner of Indian Affairs, Cato Sells:

> 'I was with the Turkey Leg band when the treaty was signed at the Red Cloud agency in 1876 and I was present when the treaty was made, but the Black Hills were not sold by that treaty. The Black Hills were just leased to the Government and the white people allowed to mine the gold, the Indians to get half and the whites to get the other half of all the minerals mined...
>
> Most of the Cheyenne were away at that time and did not know anything about the signing of the treaty ...'

Big Horse, another Cheyenne, also stated in 1918:

> 'I was with the hostile camp of the Cheyenne which left the agency in the early fall before the Custer fight ...
>
> While we were away a commission came to the agency...
>
> It wished the Indians to make a treaty to permit the whites to mine the gold and for that privilege the Indians were to get one half of the gold mined ... but the Indians did not sell the country.
>
> We in the hostile camp did not authorize the agency band of Cheyenne to make a treaty and there was no talk of the Black Hills treaty before we left.'

Many other Cheyenne warriors also made such statements at that time, all to no effect and, needless to say, none of the Indians ever received any gratuities from the gold that was subsequently extracted.

Such glib practices certainly confused and worried the agency chiefs. Red Cloud and Spotted Tail were two of the most prominent Indians on the reservations and within three weeks of the commissioner's departure, Red Cloud knew that the day of the red man had gone forever. Colonel Ranald Mackenzie had left Fort Robinson in Nebraska, with eight companies of cavalry to escort all Red Cloud and Spotted Tail's people back to the fort. On arrival at the reservations, Mackenzie impounded any remaining Indian ponies, relieved the Indians of any weapons, dismantled their tipis and, after placing all male Indians under arrest, marched away every Indian back to Fort Robinson, where they were confined under the auspices of armed soldiers. This was a period where life on the frontier was hard and the region perilous to occupy. With so many hostiles still roaming the hills and valleys, military authorities may have thought it prudent to confine all Indians they could lay their hands on and, of course, agency Indians were a soft target. Whatever the reasons may have been, such treatment was certainly harsh, virtual physical and mental abuse, which only fired further resentment within the Indians for many years to come. In his last State of the Union Address, 5th December 1876, Grant grimly stated:

> 'A policy has been adopted toward the Indian tribes inhabiting a large portion of the territory of the United States which has been humane and has substantially ended the Indian hostilities in the whole land except a portion of Nebraska and Dakota, Wyoming and Montana Territories, the Black Hills region and approaches there to. Hostilities there have grown out of the avarice of the white man, who had violated our treaty stipulations in his search for gold …
>
> All difficulty in this matter has, however, been removed (subject to the approval of Congress) to a treaty ceding the Black Hills and approaches to the settlement by citizens.'

Grant does not define what he considers a 'humane policy' towards the Indians and he also states that the troops were stopped from removing the prospectors from the Black Hills from fear that they might desert. He clearly had no conception of either the land in dispute or life within the frontier itself, much less the actual terms of the treaties, for he continues:

> 'The subject of Indian Policy and treatment so fully set forth by the secretary of the interior and the Commission of Indian Affairs, and my views so fully expressed therein, that I refer to their reports and recommendations as my own.'

Grant had begun his speech by admitting that errors of judgement must have occurred throughout his term as president. It is doubtful that he would ever have considered the consequences of these errors of judgement or how they would affect the lives of the Indians and the soldiers who fought them. Congress would ratify the treaty of 1876 by passing the Black Hills Act on 29th February 1877.

The Sioux and Cheyenne were totally oblivious of the furore their spectacular defeat of Custer at the Little Big Horn had caused, much less the depths to which corrupt politicians and military commanders would stoop. They would not have envisaged the ultimate results that their bid for freedom would have on their future generations. Their overwhelming victory had given them a false hope of survival against the never-ending invasion of the white men and instead of gaining sympathy for their cause, the Sioux and Cheyenne had, in effect, initiated the reverse. Unfortunately for them, the Indians had made three crucial mistakes that summer: they had won a tremendous victory against a national hero; they had killed him in the process; and they had been victorious at the wrong time, when the nation was in the midst of celebrating its centennial. Revulsion at the news of Custer's death swept across the country like a bush fire. On 7th July the *Chicago Tribune* wrote:

> 'It is time to quit this Sunday-school policy, and let Sheridan recruit regiments of western pioneer hunters and scouts, and exterminate every Indian who will not remain upon the reservations.
>
> The best use to make of an Indian who will not stay on a reservation is to kill him.
>
> It is time that the dawdling, maudlin peace-policy was abandoned.'

Fortunately, not all newspapers shared the same sentiments. On 12th July *The New York Times* stated:

> '... It is even desirable that our defeats should impel us to wage war in the sharp, vigorous manner which is the truest mercy to friend and foe. But is neither just nor decent that a Christian nation yield itself to homicidal frenzy, and clamour for the instant extermination of savages by whose unexpected bravery we have been so sadly baffled.'

Advocating temperate restraint against a frenzied revenge, *The New York Times* continued:

> 'All through the west there is manifested a wild desire for vengeance against the so-called murderers of our soldiers. The press echoes with more or less shamelessness the frontier theory that the only use to which an Indian can be put is to kill him…
>
> and public opinion, not only in the west, but to some extent in the east, has apparently decided that the Indians have exhausted the forbearance of heaven and earth, and must now be exterminated as though they were so many mad dogs.
>
> … We must beat the Sioux, but we need not exterminate them.'

News of Custer's defeat had also reached the far shores of Europe. In London, 'The Times' was more forthright in laying the blame directly on the shoulders of the American politicians, for on 7th July it wrote:

> 'So heavy a blow has seldom, indeed, been struck at the regular troops of a civilized power by a barbarous enemy… We cannot doubt that the recital will kindle a flame in the United States before which the Indians will be driven back upon the alternative of death or deserts more barren and distant even than those of the present 'reserves'.
>
> The people of the United States, and especially the men of the west, who alone in this generation have been brought into actual contact with the Red Indians, have under the influence of those humanitarian ideas which are found to plead so powerfully for a mollification of English policy when we have to deal with inferior races. The conduct of the American Government towards the Indians of the plains has been neither very kind nor very wise…
>
> The borderers will certainly make the disaster to General Custer's command an excuse for forcing upon the Government a war of extermination or expulsion.'

Less than three years later British soldiers would face a similar disaster at Isandlwana and the Zulu nation would suffer as a consequence of their victory. Another war, in another place, at another time, but its reasons and actions are so familiar! Thus, it was obvious to all for the Sioux and Cheyenne that the price of victory would be extremely high.

Indian accounts for this period are almost non-existent and of those that can be found, the historian should view them with circumspection. However, if they are examined with caution, they do present the movements of the hostiles fairly accurately.

On abandoning their encampments, situated on the west bank of the Little Big Horn, the triumphant but weary Indians turned towards the south-west and the protection of the Big Horn Mountains, firing the grass behind them to delay any pursuit. They paused only once, during the night of 26th June, for a few hours before continuing their journey. For the wounded they carried their movements must have been excruciatingly painful but circumstances dictated the pace, for their scouts had brought news that fresh soldiers were approaching from the north. It was the impending arrival of the Terry/Gibbon column that had prompted the hostiles to abandon the fight with Reno and his troops. It was time to move out. The following day they pushed on, slowly traversing through the valley, but always staying close to the cool, clear water of the river. Maintaining a steady water supply was a basic necessity and here, as accounts are a little unclear, it is assumed that on reaching the confluence of Lodge Grass Creek with the Little Big Horn, the Indians changed course to follow the tributary and that night they ground to a halt, just three kilometres [just under two miles] below the mouth of the creek. Here, under the shadow of the mountains, Sitting Bull decided to give his followers a well- earned rest and a chance to recount their heroic deeds, although for some it was a time of mourning.

The evening of the 27th June was warm with clear summer skies. It was the perfect weather in which to hold a victory dance. Their spirits were high and the hostiles exuded confidence, something they had not done in a long while. They had no fear of the soldiers for the present and casting their inhibitions to the wind, the Sioux and Cheyenne settled down to the serious business of celebrating their victory. It was the most magnificent spectacle that any of the warriors had ever witnessed and it was to be one that would never be repeated. Huge fires spread their flames into the night sky, crackling and spitting glowing embers, making the shadows of the dancing warriors gesticulate grotesquely on the sides of the surrounding lodges. Rawhide drums beat out a steady rhythm in tandem with the Indians as they danced and whooped throughout the night. They had fought two major battles with the hated soldiers and they were alive to tell the tale, stories of heroic deeds that would be told and retold to each new generation. For one warrior in particular, it was a celebration of personal triumph, although he found it painfully difficult to participate due to a wound he had sustained whilst fighting Custer's soldiers on the ridge. In only than a few hours, White Bull had counted seven coups, killed two soldiers in actual physical combat, taken two guns from the field and captured no less than twelve cavalry mounts. Such bravery in the face of the enemy was difficult to equal and his achievement had not gone unnoticed, for songs of his exploits were already being sung this night in his honour.

A nephew of Sitting Bull, White Bull would later become chief of the Miniconjou Sioux, whilst his brother, One Bull, who had been adopted by Sitting Bull, would become chief of the Hunkpapa Sioux. Both men had distinguished themselves as warriors in battle and were held with great respect by their people. One Bull died on 23rd June 1947 at the age of 94. Just over a month later, on 26th July, White Bull died aged 98.

The huge assemblage of Sioux and Cheyenne remained in the area of Lodge Grass Creek for about a week. The abundance of game ensured they were fed and clothed, whilst the nearby forests that adorned the lower slopes of the Big Horn Mountains, served to replace old or damaged lodge poles. It was a euphoric existence, but it could not last. Each day they remained there brought the possibility of discovery by the soldiers even closer. They had to move on or become trapped.

On or around 7th July, the hostiles broke camp and headed north-east, travelling back towards the valley of the Little Big Horn, crossing the river and moving on towards the Rosebud. Here they stopped for a few days to replenish their supplies before crossing the Tongue to make camp on Blue Stone Creek, a tributary of the Powder River. As they slowly traversed eastwards, the Indians set fire to the grassy plain behind them as they had always done at this time of year and for the next few weeks the whole area between the Big Horn and Powder rivers was shrouded in thick black smoke, crazily billowing towards the sky. Even the forests on the Big Horn Mountains were ablaze and by the time the early autumn rains had fallen, the whole region had become nothing more than a black dismal wilderness, totally inhospitable to man and beast and a far cry from the wild beautiful country that the Indians had entered earlier.

Here, by the cool clear running water of Blue Stone Creek, the Sioux and Cheyenne parted company to go their separate ways. Sitting Bull and the Sioux continued their progress north-eastwards towards Pumpkin Creek, while Two Moon and the Cheyenne swung south-east towards the Powder.

According to Cheyenne accounts, on reaching the Powder River another of their warriors died from wounds he had received at the Little Big Horn, bringing their losses up to seven. (This cannot be taken as the absolute truth as the Indians did not keep records of their killed and wounded.) The Cheyenne knew this region well. Water was readily available and there was an abundance of game. But their stay by the Powder was short, as they had to keep moving to avoid contact with the soldiers. It was hardly three weeks since their fight with the soldiers at the Little Big Horn and they did not know that the soldiers were not scouring the region for them at that moment. Turning northwards, the Cheyenne crossed Mizpah Creek heading towards the Yellowstone. Just north of Pumpkin Creek the Sioux and Cheyenne joined forces again. Whether this reunion was intentional or by chance is not known, however this particular area was the usual autumn hunting grounds of both nations at various times, so it would not be unreasonable to assume that Sitting Bull had allowed his people to linger here to replenish provisions. The huge Sioux encampment would not be difficult for the Cheyenne to find.

It had taken the hostiles just over a month to travel this far and for some days now a few warriors, here and there, had left the meandering hoards to return to their respective agencies. Autumn had set in and the following winter months could be incredibly harsh in this region. Thus, these warriors believed they could return to the agency to be fed and clothed by the government during the winter months and then abscond into the hills once more when spring arrived. They had no idea that they would be held responsible for the deaths of Custer and his men, for the army had failed to find them so far, allowing them to believe they had won a victory in a fair fight. It was not unreasonable then for the Indians to reach this conclusion, after all they had only defended their families. In any event, it was on conversing with warriors such as these that Captain Poland obtained the valuable information that he dutifully sent to Sheridan on 24th July, giving the route the Indians were following:

> '… followed, towards and along the base of the Rosebud Mountains.'

Poland's information was extremely accurate, but Sheridan ignored his letter thus losing valuable time as well as the hostile Indians. Was this deliberate? It does appear so. Sheridan had to cover all the trails and he needed time to do that. In actual fact, once Crook was on the move again, he crossed the Indians' trail just south of the Rosebud and even though it was a month old, he followed it until his meeting with Terry. If Crook had moved at an earlier date he would have run straight into the hostiles and would probably have changed the course of history.

By early August, the Indians had reached Cherry Creek, just north of the Yellowstone where, once again, the Sioux and Cheyenne parted company. Two Moon took the Cheyenne back southwards towards the lower regions of the Powder. Sitting Bull and the Sioux also re-crossed the Yellowstone, although they continued to follow the river northwards for some distance before they too split up leaving Sitting Bull and his followers to head towards the Killdeer Mountains in North Dakota, whilst Low Dog headed north towards Canada with some of the Oglala Sioux. It is assumed that the Arapaho, who had also participated at the Little Big Horn, remained with Sitting Bull as their movements during this time are unclear.

It is quite obvious that due to the army's inaction, the Sioux and Cheyenne were able to move quite freely across the region and put some considerable distance between themselves and the Little Big Horn. However, Sitting Bull and his war chiefs were no fools. They must have been aware of the soldiers' locations and of the fact that they had not immediately mobilised to hunt them down. Their own scouts would have reported any such movements without delay. In fact, the hostiles were so confident at this point that they moved their people directly between the forces of Terry and Crook as they headed north–east in July! Why were they not defeated? Terry and Crook had scouts out, so why were they missed? A huge number of people on the move and no one saw them? Perhaps the army did not want to find them right now.

The lull was only temporary and news of the army resuming the campaign was swift in reaching the hostiles. Across the region, by smoke signal and swift-footed runners, came the news that the soldiers were on the offensive again. For the hostiles, the news was ominous although not unduly critical. With some warriors leaving for the agencies, their manpower was dwindling and even with the captured arms and ammunition from the Custer fight, they did not have enough to engage the soldiers to be sure of winning a second time. The military appeared to have an endless supply of weapons and ammunition, and no matter how many soldiers the hostiles killed there were hundreds more to take their place. For the present, the frontier would witness a game of 'cat and mouse' and for the hostiles it would mean evading the enemy at all costs whilst they replenished their supplies. Winter was not a good time of the year for the Indians to engage in any kind of conflict. Sitting Bull had no intention of surrendering and he urged his followers to stand firm. When he met Colonel Nelson Miles a few weeks later he adamantly stated:

> 'Almighty God made me an Indian, but not an agency Indian!'

The military, however, had other ideas.

Crook crossed the lower reaches of the Tongue and began his march northward towards the Rosebud. The march was arduous and the rough terrain proved a problem for the infantry who had to continuously wade through rivers and the tributaries that fed them. Unlike the cavalry, whose mounts had no problem striding through the water, the infantry occasionally found themselves waist deep and on reaching the Tongue, had to recross it several times to maintain their line of march. However, Crook's troops buzzed with an air of excitement on being back in the campaign. Sergeant John Powers of the 5th Cavalry, who had recently joined Crook's forces from Fort Hayes in Kansas, wrote:

> 'We were, to believe all accounts, going right down into Mr Sitting Bull's camp and eat him up without salt.'

The night-time bivouac posed problems for all the troops. Having no change of clothing, the troops slept in the same clothes for days on end and used their saddle blankets to roll up in. The pungent aroma of an army on campaign could not have been very sweet. Ants were another problem, crawling inside the soldier's clothes and inflicting bites. Then there was the rain, which soaked the soldiers to their skin. On 12th August, Private William Jordan of the 14th Infantry wrote:

> 'Has rained steadily for forty-eight hours. In camp. No shelter of any kind. Stood up all night with blankets over our shoulders, and soaking wet.'

By 7th August Crook had reached the Rosebud, where he found a huge Indian trail that appeared to be heading north-east. The month-old trail was so wide that many of Crook's men viewed it with awe. Private James Frew, 5th Cavalry, noted:

> '... a very heavy Indian trail. Like a road.'

Infantry Private Howard was more descriptive:

> '...a big square...having wounded warriors on travois.'

From this last comment it appears that the soldiers did not conceive the possibility that the hostiles would be travelling with their families, they just thought they were in pursuit of warriors. Thus, the travois marks on the trail had to be wounded warriors and not Indian family bundles, etc.

The Indian trail followed the Rosebud for some considerable distance and Crook turned his forces to pick up the trail. However, any possibility that Crook would actually find the hostiles, much less engage them, was extremely remote, even though signs of Indian habitation increased as the column slowly edged forwards. From written accounts it appears that the hostiles had used the same trail to depart from the Little Big Horn as when they were heading towards it. Private Howard described the debris they encountered, which gave the impression that a Sun Dance had been held along the trail:

> 'There were six buffalo heads collected in the ring and a war pole in the centre smeared with blood.'

Soldiers of Custer's forces also noted much of the same debris as they passed along the trail earlier in June. Private Howard also recorded fresh Indian signs:

> 'Went past several rather fresh Indian graves...'

Indian graves were a magnet to soldiers, who delighted in looting them. Campaigns on the whole were laborious and boring, especially if the troops covered hundreds of kilometres without even sighting a hostile Indian, let alone fighting one. Of course, it does not condone the practice for it was nothing less than grave robbing, but Indian trophies were all many soldiers had to show for their actions on the frontier, even if their trophies were stripped from the dead. In the abandoned Indian encampment on the Little Big Horn, blankets and buffalo robes were taken from the dead warriors that were found, many of which became bedding for the seventh's wounded. However, in most cases Indian trophies consisted of moccasins, pipes, charms, and other fetishes, all of which could fetch a good price in the townships, if the owner wished to sell them. Later in the campaign, deserted or destroyed Indian camps also revealed their participation in the fight when military articles were discovered, such as axes and coffee mills lying alongside blood-soaked stone hammers. Private William Taylor, Company A, 7th Cavalry, was not opposed to collecting Indian trophies either. In his memoirs of his part in the Little Big Horn campaign, he mentions two Indian arrows that he acquired:

> 'One body was nude like all the rest and in it were several arrows, two of which I pulled out and brought away.'

As Taylor was describing the burials of Custer's command, it can be safely assumed that the body he refers to was that of a soldier, so it was not only the Indian dead that was looted! Not that many years ago two of Taylor's other trophies have come under the hammer at auction, one of which caused some concern under the Native American Graves Protection and Repatriation Act, and has undergone scientific examination by the Federal Bureau of Investigation. The first item was a pipe/tomahawk that had a faded label attached bearing the date of 19 August, 1876. The auction catalogue listed the pipe/tomahawk as an artefact from the battle of Slim Buttes, but it is doubtful that it is as the label pre-dates the battle of Slim Buttes which took place on 8th September 1876. However, it is the second item that had caused concern as it is a cultural item of human remains, being a braided scalp decorated with a covering of red wool and a contrasting blue wool cross. Scientific examination of the artefact by the F.B.I. has revealed that,

> '… the hair on the scalp exhibits mongoloid characteristics, a classification that encompasses Native American hair.'

In 2002, representatives of the native Indian tribes reviewed the report and concluded that the item was probably a scalp taken by one of the Sioux tribes of a traditional enemy, thus the scalp is innately sacred and comes under the Native American Graves Protection and Repatriation Act. It has, in all likelihood, been returned to the Indians, assuming that no other claimant has come forward. How or where Taylor obtained those items is not clear, although it is generally believed that he did acquire them after the battle of Slim Buttes, September 1876.

As Crook and his command continued to follow the Indian trail, Terry also mobilised his troops. On 1st August his forces had been re-enforced by six companies of the 22nd Infantry under the command of Lieutenant

Colonel Otis and the following day, Colonel Nelson Miles arrived with six companies of the 5th Infantry. It is obvious to even a greenhorn that neither Terry nor Crook had any wish to actually face the hostiles, as infantry are no match for Indians.

Nelson Miles was as near to a carbon copy of George Custer as one could get. At the onset of the Civil War he was a 22-year-old clerk in a goods store but, unlike Custer, he did not go to West Point to obtain his commission. He purchased it instead. Nonetheless, Miles was intensely ambitious and by 1865 he had attained the rank of brevet major general, this being commuted to colonel when he took command of the 5th Infantry in Kansas. He married Sherman's niece, Mary, which many perceived as a social or promotional move, but in actual fact he did love her and dutifully wrote to her every night throughout his numerous campaigns. It is generally believed that he did use his family connection to pressure Sherman to allow him a strike at the Sioux and he was rewarded by being assigned to Terry. It was not exactly what he had hoped for but, like Terry, he had to accept what he could get and it did put him in the area of the Sioux, where he had the possibility of some action. Miles drove his troops up to and beyond the call of duty, believing that if he was capable of achieving a good result, then so were his men. In August 1874 he had commanded a column of about 700 men in a running chase after some Kiowa Indians, a chase that continued for over thirty-two kilometres (just under twenty miles). The heat had been so intense that in some places the temperature reached 110 degrees fahrenheit in the shade! Needless to say, the Kiowa were run into the ground and captured, but it took several weeks for his men to recover from the ordeal. Miles was tough and where Custer had apparently failed, he was determined to succeed. In later years, Miles wrote of the Sioux campaign:

> '....Every single man under my command realised the desperate nature of this encounter.
>
> ...Every officer and soldier knew that a mistake meant annihilation and we therefore inspired to deeds of heroism and fortitude.'

Terry had requested additional cavalry to boost his command, having already experienced the pitfalls of employing infantry to pursue Indians. His request was not granted and he had to make do with extra foot soldiers instead. Sheridan and Sherman could not allow the hostiles to be caught so soon! It was easier to be obtuse than downright stupid. In any event, on

8th August Terry sallied forth leading a force of approximately 1,700 men, down the Rosebud. At his disposal he had four infantry battalions, comprising of the 5th, 6th, 7th, and 22nd Infantry Regiments, all under the overall command of Colonel Gibbon and four companies of the 2nd Cavalry, plus what remained of the Seventh, under the command of Major Brisbin. The terrain was particularly difficult to cross and the recent heavy rainfalls made their progress hazardous and painfully slow. Thus, it was not until the 10th August, two days later, that Terry finally joined forces with Crook at a bend in the river.

Whilst Terry and Crook retired to consider their next move, the troops settled into camp with many taking the opportunity to wash their threadbare uniforms and take a much needed bath in the freezing water of the Rosebud. Both Terry and Crook knew that the hostile Indians had eluded them and they were also aware that their troops were very demoralised with the whole campaign. Gibbon later wrote:

> 'General Crook's column was on a large Indian trail which had been followed for some distance down the Rosebud. Just where our two forces joined, the trail left the valley of the Rosebud, and turned eastwards towards the Tongue River.'

As their scouts could not agree on the age of the trail, Gibbon feared that the hostiles had actually crossed the Powder River and escaped towards the Yellowstone. If they crossed the Yellowstone they could head north and the safety of Canada. If this was the general consensus throughout the combined forces, why did the military not plan its strategy accordingly? They had already wasted too much time, remaining inactive for such a long period that the hostiles were allowed to make good their escape. In retrospect it appears that the military had, once again, misjudged the hostiles believing that they were heading for the Canadian border, when in actual fact they were merely heading for their usual wintering sites and dispersing accordingly to their tribe or nation en route. They were cleverly out-manoeuvring the soldiers by keeping just one step ahead of them. The Sioux had leisurely trekked across the region, the sheer size of their column had dictated the pace and had the army employed cavalry to give chase at an earlier date, the Indians would have been located and probably engaged. Yet, even now, fearing that the hostiles would escape north to Canada, the army still sat on its heels and pondered their next move, and still employed infantry!

Of course, it is possible that Sheridan had not foreseen that the campaign would last this length of time. It was now becoming very costly. To allow the hostiles to make good their plan of destroying Custer, neither Terry nor Crook could be allowed to move their forces too quickly. But even the best laid plans go awry. Terry and Crook had remained static for too long and the hostiles naturally took full advantage of this. Now the troops would have to search for them and that could take a lot of manpower and time, which amounted to an awful lot of money. Statistics produced at the time state that it cost the government $1,000,000 to kill a single Indian and that the cost of keeping a regiment in the field, on the frontier, was a staggering $2,000,000 per year! It is suspect that these figures are entirely correct, but it was certainly a costly venture to maintain over 2,000 troops on a campaign that did not seem to have an end in sight. The logistics alone must have been horrendous and the taxpayers in the east would be quick to complain. Gibbon wrote:

> 'During their six month's absence in the field the objects attained by them were not at all proportionate to the efforts put forth, but should any feel inclined to criticize too closely our want of success by indulging in sarcastic calculations as to how many millions of dollars are required to kill one Indian, the only answer can be made is—the truth of which is well recognized by the army—that war is far more costly than peace, and that it has never been, and never can be, a paying speculation …
>
> … it may be safely asserted that, considering the circumstances, Indian wars are in proportion no more costly than any other kind of wars.'

Nevertheless, on 11th August Terry and Crook resumed the march, following the Indian trail towards the junction of the Powder with the Yellowstone. Having sent their supply train, under an escort of the 5th Infantry, back to the Yellowstone, the combined forces were now relying solely on the pack mules for their provisions. The generals had calculated that the mules would be sufficient until they reached the mouth of the Powder, where steamers could replenish their supplies. It was raining heavily as the troops trudged their way across the high rolling hills that ley between the Rosebud and the Tongue, making their journey all the more arduous and miserable. Gibbon described the rainfall:

> '... and that night, after making our bivouac under a clear sky, the rain commenced to fall in torrents, and it was not long before each man, from the General to the Private soldier, found himself lying in a pool of water...'

The heavy rain was not their only concern, however, for the soaked and shivering men were also plagued by mosquitoes and rattlesnakes. Camp sites had to be cleared of the latter every evening, with snake bites becoming a common feature. By the time the forces reached the Powder, on 15th August, the men were tired, hungry, and very irritable. Relations between Terry and Crook had deteriorated too which did little to ease the worsening situation. Gibbon summed up their plight when he wrote:

> 'We reached the Powder River on the 15th, after passing over a very rough broken country, only to find the whole country burnt over, and no Indians in sight.'

The soldiers reached the confluence of the Powder with the Yellowstone on 17th August. Morale was extremely low and even the Crow scouts had had enough. The Indian trail they had been following suddenly veered off towards the east, although the scouts expressed doubt any continuance of their pursuit would result in engaging the hostiles, so it was abandoned. Supplies were running seriously low and the animals were suffering terribly from the lack of any forage. Gibbon wrote:

> 'The mouth of the Powder is a black, desolate region with poor grass, much of which had been burnt off by the Indians ...'

Terry and Crook remained at the mouth of the Powder for the next seven days, during which time the steamers continued to deliver the much needed supplies and with the steamers came the sutlers, eager to ply their trade. To Crook's troops, who had steadily marched overland and had to rely on wagons and mules for their supplies, the steamers were a welcome sight. In addition to the large steamers, small packet boats brought further provisions and some re-enforcements, but it was the sutlers who exacted the most trade. Apart from the substandard whiskey that they sold for exorbitant prices, the sutlers also sold canned and bottled foods, fresh vegetables, tobacco, and clothing. Of course it was a cash only trade, which severely limited the enlisted men and the goods on offer were not always fresh, but the sutlers did very well all the same.

So far the summer campaign of 1876 had been a complete and utter disaster as far as the public were concerned. Custer and a large portion of his command had been killed; numerous soldiers had been terribly wounded, with many falling seriously ill; public money was being spent to maintain the soldiers in the field; and there had been nothing to show for it at all, absolutely nothing, not one living hostile Indian had been seen since the battle, much less captured or killed. Terry and Crook were well aware that their troops were very demoralised, but other than to resume the search neither could provide an instant solution. On 20th August the Crow scouts left the command to return to their families and prepare for the winter. They had performed incredible work, which has not always been recognised over the years, but they too were disappointed in not being able to locate the Sioux or Cheyenne. A few days later, when the march had resumed, Gibbon noted just how valuable the Crows' service had been:

> 'Now it was that we felt the great want of our Crow allies, for this region of country was totally unknown to us.'

But the search for the hostiles was not over. Far from it.

Chapter 3

Revelations

Having fully recuperated from their ordeal, the troops took to the trail again on 24th August. The following day news reached Terry and Crook that steamers carrying more re-enforcements had been fired on by Indians further down the Yellowstone. Whether these were Sioux or Cheyenne has not been determined. Before leaving the Powder River they had received reports that Indians were crossing the river near Fort Buford, so it was now assumed that the hostiles were endeavouring to escape to the north. Terry and Crook decided to dispatch the 6th Infantry to investigate the reports and patrol the Yellowstone, thus reducing their command. There does not appear to be any concern regarding the strength of the hostiles any more, even though the signs still showed they were of a considerable number. Two days later, having reached the Yellowstone near the mouth of O'Fallon Creek, Terry and Crook decided to part company and continue the search as independent forces. It was a strange decision considering they knew the area abounded with signs of recent hostile activity, although it was unclear in which direction the main body had gone. Crook chose to push south, then east, leaving Terry to continue his march to the north.

The following day, 27th August, steamers ferried Terry's command across the Yellowstone and after securing fresh supplies on pack mules, the troops began the gloomy prospect of a night march towards Upper Seven Mile Creek. Looming ahead of them were the Big Sheep Mountain ranges, beyond which lay Redwater River, a tributary of the Missouri. Terry did not have any scouts that were familiar with the area and those he had were doubtful whether or not they would find fresh water. Gibbon wrote:

> 'The peninsular lying between the Missouri and Yellowstone rivers, here something over one hundred miles [approximately 160 kilometres] wide, is known to be a high rolling divide, intersected by but few streams, and these generally dry in summer.'

Due west of the mountains was Big Dry Creek, another tributary of the Missouri that was known to be a favourite location of the Sioux during the winter months and a lodge pole was known to exist there. It was not unreasonable for Terry to assume that if the hostiles had already crossed the Yellowstone, they would probably use this old trail and winter by the creek. Again, his subsequent movements indicate that Terry did not really want to engage the hostiles, for he did not head in that direction. It could be argued that Terry did not have enough supplies for his troops to undertake such a lengthy journey, whether there were hostiles sheltering there or not. In any event, he was not prepared to take the chance.

The march continued well into the night before Terry finally ordered a halt. The troops settled down totally exhausted, but their break was short lived for Terry resumed the march in the early hours of the morning, before anyone even had breakfast. Was this a show of encouragement on Terry's behalf or petulance, for he had heard the grumbling from the ranks. The recent rainfalls had allowed the grass to grow lush and green, giving the soldiers hope of finding fresh water. But it was only to be found in the form of large pools. Terry halted the command and allowed the troops to prepare breakfast. A few hours later they were on the move again, still heading due north. As the day wore on it became unbearably hot and the lack of water became a serious issue. Their scouts had returned to report they had seen buffalo and if buffalo were in the area there must also be water, possibly Indians as well. The soldiers found the buffalo, but instead of finding water or Indians they discovered gnats, big ugly buffalo gnats, which swarmed over the column stinging men and horses with impunity. It was a nightmare march and many were hoping for a speedy end to their torment. Even hostile Indians were preferable to these awful insects. There was still no sign of fresh water for the evening camp, although the horses and mules could munch on fresh, damp grass.

The following day, still heading north, the march took the command into the high rolling hills which were rich in pasture and abundant in game. Antelope pranced tantalizingly around the weary soldiers and upon reaching a high ridge, a huge herd of buffalo could be observed grazing quietly below. There was still no sign of any Indians though, so Terry halted the troops and allowed them to hunt fresh meat. Apart from being a short deviation from a tedious march, at least it ensured they all ate well that evening and it replenished their dwindling supplies. Terry must have thought long and hard that night, for his subsequent movements show that if he had any ideas that the hostiles could be found in the west, he was determined to go in the opposite direction. His search so far had proved to be a complete waste of time and it appears that it was only a token gesture anyway for the observers in the east. When the march was resumed at dawn, Terry headed due east, where again he failed to make contact with any hostiles and he must have been aware that his troops were thoroughly demoralised, as well as totally exhausted. It was obvious to all that the probability of large bodies of Indians north of the Yellowstone was unlikely and that their painful trek had all been for nothing.

By 31st August Terry had turned south, heading back towards the Yellowstone where, three days later, his command went into camp at the mouth of Glendive Creek. They had fresh water at last, but only now did the bitter truth of the situation strike home. The hostile Indians had obviously divided into smaller groups somewhere south of the Yellowstone where, at any time, they could either remain dispersed or regroup as circumstances dictated. The Indians had out-smarted and out-manoeuvred the army. Their only hope was that Crook's forces had been able to locate them. Terry had heard nothing from Crook and he had no idea where he was.

On 5th September Gibbon received his orders to return with his command to Fort Ellis in Montana. For his troops the campaign was over, but not their ordeal. Gibbon departed the following day knowing they had to retrace their steps for hundreds of kilometres along the Yellowstone, with little hope of obtaining any supplies by steamer as the river was low and virtually unnavigable. Major Brisbin and his four companies of the 2nd Cavalry reached Fort Ellis on the 29th September; with six companies of the 7th Infantry commanded by Captain Freemen arriving at Fort Shaw on 6th October. Gibbon accompanied the infantry, for on 17th October he duly submitted his report to Terry from Fort Shaw. His report was very descriptive of his participation in the summer campaign and extremely scathing of the authorities, whom he blamed for their failure to locate the hostiles, in particular the army medical department:

> 'In addition to our other wants, we were entirely devoid of any proper means for the transportation of the sick or wounded.
>
> … As it was, a few wounded men were all—sufficient to cripple, for offensive operations, a large body of troops; for in savage warfare to leave one's wounded behind is out of the question.'

Curiously, Gibbon does not expand on the subject of cavalry versus infantry for such operations, for he must have realised that the use of cavalry when in pursuit of Indians would have been far more practicable. However, he does extol the efforts of his command, for he concludes his report with:

> 'During the summer's operations the cavalry marched nearly 1,500 miles [2,414 kilometres] and the infantry nearly 1,700 miles [2,736 kilometres], beside some 900 miles [1,448 kilometres] by portions of cavalry and 500 miles [805 kilometres] by portions of the infantry in scouting and escort duty.'

Of course, such a statement does leave the historian wondering how Gibbon actually arrived at these figures, for they are far too nicely rounded to be totally accurate. However, they do give the impression that his troops did cover very large areas during the campaign, under extremely difficult conditions, with a relentless effort in accordance with their orders and all to no avail, which in all probability, the general idea.

For General Alfred Terry the campaign was all but over and, if the truth be told, he was probably more relieved than anyone else. There is no doubt that the carnage of the battle deeply shocked him and he had no wish to see such dreadful sights again. He had established a camp at the mouth of Glendive Creek, where the supply steamers could still just about reach him, along the Yellowstone. On 26th August Terry received orders from Sheridan to create a base camp at the mouth of the Tongue, where troops could patrol the Yellowstone Valley. In compliance with his orders, Terry placed Colonel Miles and the 5th Infantry at the depot, along with Lieutenant Colonel Otis and his 22nd Infantry. The accumulation of enough supplies for these troops to survive the winter was not an easy task. The steamers had managed to reach Glendive Creek with supplies, but three of them had run aground and thus it fell to Miles and his command to transport what supplies they could to their camp on the Tongue. Terry must have harboured serious doubts concerning the planning of the campaign, but he never aired them, at least not in public. On 16th September Terry left Glendive Creek and returned to his headquarters in St. Paul. He never again took to the field during the remaining years of the Indian Wars.

Further afield, George Crook was doggedly pursuing his quarry. His command had fared no better than Terry's, in fact Crook's troops would experience much more worsening conditions before they were allowed to quit the field. Upon his departure from Terry, Crook moved south then turned towards the east, moving forward to the valley of the Little Missouri River. What followed next has been described as the 'mud march', the 'horse-meat march' and the 'starvation march', but whatever term is selected, it was an arduous march that pushed the soldiers way beyond their physical and mental capabilities, almost to the death. Crook had abandoned his supply wagons when he bid farewell at O'Fallon Creek, relying on pack mules to transport his supplies. In addition, he ordered his troops to discard any extra clothing, all tent equipment, and all unnecessary articles. They would be travelling light.

Right from the start heavy rain hampered their progress, turning the soil into wet sticky mud that drained the strength of both men and animals. The rain continued as they trudged across the Badlands, from Montana to North Dakota. Horses, mules, and men slid in the quagmires, their bodies already soaked by the rain became saturated with slimy mud. There was no relief during the night camps either, for having no tents the troops had to improvise with their blankets draped over branches. By the time the command had reached the Little Missouri rations were running low and Crook ordered that their daily intake must be cut in half. The troops foraged from the land as best as they could, but it was not enough to subsidise their daily allowance of two crackers, a half ration of coffee and any other food the soldiers had reserved in their saddlebags. Corporal John Zimmerman of Company I, 14th Infantry recalled:

> 'Each man had one quart cup, no other cooking utensil, he toasted his bacon or ate it raw. Boiled his coffee in the cup and drank it from the same, making it strong or weak as far as the coffee would go.'

After two weeks of tortuous marching, the troops' hunger turned to starvation. Depression at having to endure such deprivations was gnawing away at many soldiers and the symptoms of scurvy were rearing their ugly heads. The rain was still impeding their movements and there had been no sign to indicate that any Indian life was in the vicinity. Morale had reached an all-time low. Company officers were becoming increasingly alarmed, not only for the physical well-being of their troops but also the growing discord within the ranks. On raising their concerns to Crook, the order was passed down to shoot all lame or exhausted horses and mules for issue as meat rations. Private Thomas Lloyd of Company E, 3rd Cavalry wrote:

> 'I don't mind the fighting part, but the hardships…
> … and the starvation.
> …as soon as you would get to camp, shoot an old sore-back mule, so poor he could hardly walk, take your butcher knife, cut as nice slice as you could get and eat it raw. No salt, pepper nor anything at all…'

Aware of the dreadful condition of his men, Crook had no alternative but to abandon the search and return to civilisation. On reaching an area roughly central between the Killdeer Mountains and Rainy Buttes, Crook turned the column and headed south towards the Black Hills. His soldiers were not even sure whether they could endure the distance. In an effort to boost morale, Crook sent messengers to telegraph Sheridan requesting supplies of grain, meat and fresh vegetables be in readiness to meet them at Deadwood, in South Dakota. As the column slowly pushed on, conditions deteriorated even further. Soldiers barely able to walk with their swollen legs left a trail of blood from their bleeding feet. What had begun as a chase had turned into a struggle for survival. Many who had been pushed beyond their limit of endurance sat down and cried, only managing to struggle to their feet on being implored to do so by their friends, who were also at their limits. To fall by the wayside meant certain death. At least there was hope of salvation if they kept moving. One member of Crook's force wrote later that he had seen,

> 'men so exhausted that they were actually insane.'

Unbeknown to Crook, his change of direction was actually taking him into the region many of the hostiles had chosen for their winter camp. Sitting Bull was camped on the Grand River near Twin Buttes, with around 1,000 seasoned warriors. Further south, American Horse was camped near Slim Buttes, with thirty-seven lodges of Miniconjou Sioux. He was intending to move on to the Spotted Tail agency, where he naively assumed his people would be welcome to stay throughout the winter months. A little further east near Antelope Buttes, there was a large camp of circles of Sans Arc, Cheyenne, and Oglala under Crazy Horse, who were already settled in their autumn locations ready to trade with neighbouring tribes and hunt meat for the winter. What were Crook's scouts doing leading the soldiers into this hornets' nest? If Crook had been aware of the close proximity of the hostiles, he would have faced a serious dilemma, for approximately two-thirds of his command were unfit for duty.

By 7th September, Crook had reached the north fork of the Grand River and the situation within his command had become desperate. The mining town of Deadwood lay roughly 160 kilometres [99.4 miles] due south in the Black Hills. Relief for the troops was so near and yet so far. Many had already collapsed unable to endure the suffering any longer and were having to be carried on litters. Crook instructed Captain Anson Mills and 150 soldiers of the 3rd Cavalry, who still had serviceable mounts, to escort sixty-one of the remaining mules to advance into Deadwood and purchase anything they could lay their hands on and bring the supplies back to the column.

Two days later, on 9th September, at the crack of dawn, Mills inadvertently stumbled upon the Miniconjou village of American Horse, situated on Rabbit Creek by the pine covered slopes of Slim Buttes. Although he and his men were absolutely exhausted, Mills attacked at once taking the Indians by surprise and within a short time he had secured the village, driving the Indians on to the surrounding bluffs. Mills did not have enough men to maintain the pressure, so he sent a courier back to Crook to inform him of his disposition. Crook hurried forward as quickly as he could. No doubt the news of Mills' engagement with the hostiles spurred the men on, whatever their condition. On reaching the village that evening Crook found that Mills had everything under control. At the far end of the camp, thick with box elder, a few warriors who were accompanied by fifteen women and several children, had taken refuge in a cave and were returning fire on the soldiers who had pinned them down. The hostiles were doggedly determined to make a fight of it and by the time Crook had appeared on the scene, they had succeeded in killing Mills' scout Buffalo Chips Charley, a trooper, and wounding nine others including Lieutenant Adolphus von Leuttwitz, whose shattered leg had to be amputated. Crook positioned his forces along the canyon so they could fire a continuous volley into the entrance of the cave, to which the hostiles replied with a steady volley of their own. It was a stalemate.

A few hours later Crook called a halt to the firing as he could not see they were achieving anything. He instructed one of his scouts, Frank Grouard, to ask the hostiles to surrender. They refused, so Crook ordered the troops to resume firing into the cave and then waited. He had no idea of the strength of the trapped Indians at that time and he would not risk the lives of his men in any attempt to dislodge them. As the evening grew darker and turned to night, Crook ordered another cease fire and again instructed Grouard to request the Indians to surrender. This time Grouard was successful.

Amidst the darkening shadows of the canyon, two warriors slowly emerged from the entrance supporting a gravely wounded warrior between them. The abdomen of the wounded warrior had been ripped open by the soldier's bullets and he was clutching his entrails between his hands, blood streaming between his fingers. Holding out a bloody hand, the warrior handed his rifle over to Crook before slowly and painfully making his way back to the village. The remainder of the refugees followed meekly behind him and upon inspection, the troops found two other warriors lying in the cave already dead.

The soldiers accompanied the small band of Indians back to the village where Crook's forces had set up camp. The ageing warrior slowly lowered himself to the ground by the fire and pulled a blanket round his shoulders. Some accounts say that the warrior underwent surgery for his abdominal wound, without the relief of Chloroform, although other accounts do not confirm this. In any event, an army surgeon did examine the dreadful wound and declared it to be fatal. The warrior stayed by the fire until he eventually lost consciousness and by dawn the following day he had died. From the time he had been in the hands of the soldiers he had not uttered a single word. The courage of this warrior is beyond reproach, yet it is still not clear who he actually was. Mills had been given to believe that he had attacked a village under the leadership of American Horse and most contemporary accounts tend to agree that the fatally wounded warrior was American Horse himself. Many historians have accepted that as fact, but there are as many who have not. According to American Horse (the younger), American Horse (the elder) was not killed at Slim Buttes, but a minor chief Iron Plume (or Iron Shield). The Indian village was Miniconjou and American Horse (the elder) was a minor headman of the Miniconjou Sioux. Thus, the shadow of doubt remains as to the identity of the warrior, but whoever he was he certainly knew how to die in excruciating pain with dignity.

The Indian village had already yielded some supplies which consisted mostly of dried buffalo meat and berries. These were immediately distributed amongst the sick and wounded, with the remaining tired and famished soldiers feasting off the Indian ponies. But it was only a transient relief, starving soldiers found that this produce only staved off the pain of hunger for a few hours. On the morning of the 10th September, Crook ordered a thorough search of the village and amongst the scattered belongings of the Indians numerous military artefacts were discovered. Three horses, all bearing the brand of the Seventh Cavalry, were recovered, along with some McClellan saddles. In addition, an army officer's overcoat; an NCO blouse; a pair of army gauntlets, once the property of Captain Myles Keogh; and a Seventh Cavalry guidon of Company I, were also uncovered. These items, along with an assortment of firearms, were damning evidence in the minds of Crook's troops, that these Miniconjou Sioux had, indeed, taken part in the defeat of Custer and his men in June. Finally, they had exacted their revenge however slight.

Throughout the engagement at Slim Buttes, Crook's forces had suffered a total of fifteen casualties; three killed and twelve wounded. Unfortunately, the Indian casualties were not recorded, although it is known that many women and children were killed. Two Congressional Medals of Honour were awarded as a result of this action. For their special bravery in attempting to dislodge the hostiles from the cave the medals were awarded to Sergeant John Kirkwood and Private Robert Smith, both of whom were serving in Company M, 3rd Cavalry.

When Captain Mills launched his initial attack on the Indian village, he did not secure possession immediately which allowed many warriors to escape to neighbouring camps and raise the alarm. Crazy Horse and his Oglalas were only a few kilometres away and quickly responded to the call for help. The Oglalas arrived at Slim Buttes late in the afternoon at almost the same time as Crook and although the hostiles launched a fierce attack, Crook's troops were too formidable in number for them to press on and they had to retire to the hills. It has not been proven that Crazy Horse was actually present with the Oglala or that he took part in the attack, however, captive Indians taken by Crook's soldiers claimed that Crazy Horse had led the attack and most historians have accepted the assertions as being true. In actual fact, if the hostiles had known of the debilitated condition of the soldiers, they could have engaged Crook's command with more ferocity and inflicted enough damage for Crook to be forced to withdraw or suffer the same fate as Custer. Crazy Horse was a man to be feared. Crook on the other hand, did not have the provisions or the manpower to sustain a full scale battle and his troops must have breathed a sigh of relief when the Indians retired.

Crook buried his dead and prepared to resume the march. The internment of the dead soldiers was exacted much more carefully by Crook's men than the burials afforded Custer and his men by Terry's troops. Corporal John Zimmerman of the 14th Infantry, later described the burials at Slim Buttes:

> 'A large hole was dug in the ground right in the main trail, all of them laid in it, covered with blankets, then with canvas, filling up the hole as neatly as possible. A fire was then built on top of this, the ashes afterward scattered about the place, all the command, horses and men then marched over the spot, obliterating all signs of breaking the earth.'

In view of the fact that Crook, in all probability, would have wanted a fairly rapid withdrawal from the village, especially with talk of Crazy Horse being nearby, Zimmerman's description of the burials may have been slighted elaborated. A fire that size would have taken some hours to burn, depending on the materials used, and the ashes would have taken some time to cool down before anyone could scatter and tread them in. Hostilities had not ceased with the Indians either, who constantly fired random shots at the soldiers. However, there does appear to be little doubt that the three fatalities were given a decent burial and one that would be difficult to locate.

Crook marched his forces away from Slim Buttes, south towards Deadwood. Official reports state that nine travois and three litters were used to transport the casualties and that some hostiles made a series of attacks on the rear guard of the column, which were all repulsed. Once again, the soldiers were slogging through the slippery mud and, once again, the rain fell drenching men and animals alike. Horses and mules slid in the mud, some even falling when crossing streams, tossing their riders into the water. The constant wetness of their clothes began to take its toll on the older soldiers, who were now suffering the aches and pains of rheumatism and other related conditions. By 12th September Crook's forces literally collapsed as they reached the winding course of the Belle Fourche River, near Bear Buttes. They were only a few kilometres from Deadwood and salvation, but the men didn't care any more. They had had enough. Private Alfred McMachin of Company E, 5th Cavalry wrote:

> 'I saw that day soldiers who were a short time previously strong men, sit down by the trail in despair (sic), large, bitter tears running down their emaciated cheeks…'

Behind them the trail was littered with military items, cast away by the exhausted soldiers who did not have the strength to carry them anymore. Many of the men privately speculated whether they would even survive another day.

On 13th September the rain stopped and for the first time in weeks the soldiers could begin to dry what remained of their uniforms. Then around midday their prayers were answered. An advance party from the column that had reached Deadwood and were now returning to the main force arrived, bearing the much needed food and supplies, together with numerous citizens who had offered to help. In the forefront was a herd of cattle being pushed along by drovers and following hard on their heels were the thirteen wagons full of flour, fruit, and vegetables. Needless to say, many of the command stayed awake all through the night cooking beef and feasting on the welcome supplies. Supplies of food had arrived but nothing else. Medical supplies were critical and official reports state that typhoid was beginning to take a grip. The following day a wagon train arrived from Fort Fetterman bringing the urgently needed medical supplies, blankets, hospital tents, and fresh clothing. At long last, for the men of Crook's command their ordeal was over but it would take over a month for even the less seriously ill to recuperate from the physical effects they had suffered, whilst for many the mental effects would last forever.

Thus, the summer campaign of 1876 came to an ignominious end. Apart from those who were killed during the battle at the Little Big Horn, the only other casualties that had been incurred fighting the hostiles were those of Crook, whose overall loss had been nineteen killed and forty-two wounded. During the 'starvation march', Crook's forces had shot or abandoned 500 horses and Crook, through his own maladministration had almost killed all of his command. All in all, it had not been a very illustrious campaign and that had been due to Sheridan, more so than Terry or Crook.

For the Sioux and Cheyenne, their victorious summer was to be their last. They had pursued their dreams and won, but it was a hollow victory for the future would swallow them up in the name of progress. Other battles with the soldiers would be fought, but never again would they hold a 'victory dance' like the one they had held near Lodge Grass Creek that warm June evening. Perhaps the last word here should be left to Chief Plenty Coups, who attended a farewell address at the Little Big Horn Council in 1909, when he said:

> 'The ground on which we stand is sacred ground. It is the dust and blood of our ancestors. On these plains the Great White

Father in Washington (President Grant) sent his soldiers armed with long knives (sabres) and rifles to slay the Indians. Many of them sleep on yonder hill, where White Chief of the Long Hair (Custer) so bravely fought and fell.

A few more passing suns will see us here no more and our dust and bones will mingle with these same prairies.

I see as in a vision the dying spark of our Council fires, the ashes cold and white. I see no longer the curling smoke rising from our lodge poles. I hear no longer the songs of the women as they prepare the meal.

The antelope have gone; the buffalo willows are empty. Only the wail of the coyote is heard.

The white man's medicine is stronger than ours; his iron horse (train) rushed over the buffalo trail. He talks to us through his 'whispering spirit' (telephone).

We are like the bird with a broken wing. My heart is cold within me…'

Chapter 4

Legend or Legacy

Thus, the summer campaign of 1876 was finally over. For many of the soldiers it had been a long, hard, inglorious campaign from which they had been lucky to have escaped alive. The numerous trails they had tenaciously followed had been fraught with danger from the onset and not only from the hostile Indians, but from their own incompetent military administration. In other words, the poor bloody soldiers had survived all the horrors of the campaign in spite of their commanders, not because of them and it would be a harrowing experience that many would never forget. Those who had endured the privations of Crook's 'Starvation March', for example, would carry the indelible impressions they had witnessed, carved deep within their minds for the rest of their lives. Crook's leadership had been little short of murderous, his own self-aggrandisement being paramount of the forced marches. In short, Crook was a disgrace to the uniform and the rank he held. However, upon their return to barracks they found that word of their terrible ordeal had preceded them and they found themselves showered with concern and respect, being classed as tough old campaigners. Unfortunately for those who were still recovering in hospital, such adorations were of little consolation.

Similarly, when the survivors of the Seventh Cavalry returned to Fort Abraham Lincoln in October, they found their status as mere soldiers had also been elevated. They had suddenly become heroes and were eagerly sought after by the social circles, eager to devour every last detail the soldiers would divulge. Custer's final stand had already reached legendary proportions. Some troopers revelled in their new-found notoriety, making the most they could out of the moment, for all too soon it would be forgotten in the wake of another epic action. Others shunned such prospects, which they felt were immoral or disrespectful of the dead. These were few and far between. Then again, like Crook's troops, there were those who could not forget the dreadful spectacle they had participated in. They could still hear the war whoops of the hostiles and the deadly whizz of the arrows and bullets as the battle raged, especially during the night when all was quiet. When they closed their eyes sleep evaded their tormented souls, for they could still see the blackened and mutilated bodies of Custer and his command, decaying amidst the lush green grass on the gently rolling slopes. However much they tried, they could not erase those horrific memories and for some it became unbearable.

These men had made history. They had contributed to a legend and they had survived. However, they were a far cry from the jaunty troopers who had cheerfully followed Custer's guidon as they rode out of the fort in May. They had always said that they would follow Custer into the jaws of hell and that is exactly what they did. They had learned the hard way that life on the frontier was short and brutal, and that fighting Indians was no picnic. Thus, it was no surprise when a few soldiers resolved to accept their discharge rather than re-enlist. Such men were no cowards, they had done their duty and done it well. They just believed that they were lucky to still be alive and any further encounter with the Indians could result in being their last. They had not only discovered that Indians did not wage war as they understood it, they also faced the disturbing realisation that they had been soundly beaten.

One such soldier was First Sergeant John Ryan of Company M of the Seventh, who took his discharge in December and then returned to the east. He subsequently became a policeman in West Newton, Massachusetts, where he had been born in 1845. Here he settled and raised his family in relative obscurity. Private William Taylor, whose health had deteriorated following the campaign, accepted his discharge in January 1877. He also returned to the east, to Orange in Massachusetts, where he became a metal polisher for a sewing machine company. However, he always retained his interest in the battle on the Little Big Horn, eventually amassing many relics and leaving a plethora of information for future historians when he died in 1923.

For the officers of the Seventh, their return to the fort meant a return to the mundane life that the barracks offered. They had also experienced their moment of glory and all the torment that accompanied it. In the wake of the savage battle, they had marched their troops with Terry's relief column; rested and dutifully written their reports; then obediently followed Terry as he fruitlessly searched the wilderness for an elusive foe and they had returned to Fort Lincoln, tired, grubby, and very despondent. They had not only lost brother officers at the Little Big Horn, they had lost many friends too and they had not even been able to give them a decent burial. For the most part any discussion concerning the fight was reserved for the officer's mess or private dinner parties, after all they were officers and gentlemen. Journalists had already descended upon the fort, eager for a headline story and more were arriving daily. Custer's defeat was big news across the nation, but for the most part the officers would not disclose any information. They simply closed ranks. Custer was dead, but the regiment was still very much alive and any indiscretion now could be harmful. Some officers sought solace through releasing their emotions in letters to their families or loved ones. Captain Benteen had commenced writing to his wife upon reaching the confluence of the Big Horn with the Yellowstone and he had continued to do so on a regular basis. Obviously, such letters reassured his wife that he was unharmed, but they also allowed him to clear his conscience regarding Custer's fate as they are extremely descriptive of the operations he had been involved in. Unfortunately, Benteen did not disclose his reasons for refusing to respond to Custer's plea for help.

On the other hand, the commanding officer of the seventh, Colonel Samuel Sturgis, who until now had not taken up his duties, had no such qualms in preserving the honour of the regiment or the reputation of the man that had served as acting commander in his absence, George Custer. During an interview with one newspaper-man it is reported that he stated, in his opinion,

> 'Custer was a brave man, but a very selfish man...
>
> He was tyrannical (sic) with no regard for the soldiers under him...
>
> On the Little Big Horn he made his attack recklessly, earlier by thirty-six hours than he should have done, and with his men tired out from forced marches.'

Of course it must be remembered that Sturgis had just lost his son during the battle, so it is understandable that his feelings were running high. However, it must also be remembered that Sturgis' own career had been quite dismal by Custer's standards and, until now, he had preferred to leave the command of the regiment with his lieutenant colonel, Custer. His outburst against Custer may have been his own guilt coming to the forefront, not only his military failures but his personal failure concerning his son. In view of the fact that Sturgis failed to mention the defeat of Crook on the Rosebud or the painfully slow movements of Terry and Gibbon, his attack on Custer does appear to be of a more personal nature than a military appraisal. Even so, as a senior officer, Sturgis should not have vented such anger on Custer. It was his own opinion and he should have kept it to himself, especially when you consider that he was not fully appraised of all the facts therein.

As more and more facts became known about the battle, public opinion swayed back and forth and they snapped up any printed articles in their thirst for more information. Newspapers across the country printed their views and so-called 'first-hand accounts,' whether they were true or false, only to be discarded at a later date. Sadly, at that moment no one cared whether the articles were entirely factual. Sales were exceeding all expectations and that is what counted. Editors were inundated with letters praising their hero, absolving Custer of any blame. But there were just as many that launched scathing attacks on him, including Ulysses S. Grant who blamed Custer for the defeat. Not surprisingly it was former Confederate generals who rallied to Custer's defence, having personally experienced Custer's panache on the field of battle.

One, John McCausland, firmly attested that he would have attacked the hostiles in exactly the same way, adding,

> '... that the only way to fight with cavalry is with dash ...
> and to charge. I don't blame him at all!'

Another, Thomas L. Rosser, who had been a former classmate of Custer at West Point and a close friend, completely exonerated Custer and placed the blame for the defeat squarely on the shoulders of Major Reno, of whom he openly accused:

> '... of taking to the hills and abandoning Custer and his gallant comrades to their fate.'

It should be noted that both these men where biased towards Custer and although they had probably reacted in all sincerity, their comments only added fuel to the great debate. As for Reno, it was not the first time that he had been accused of abandoning Custer and it certainly would not be the last, much to his chagrin.

In December 1876 an Englishman by the name of Frederick Whittaker published a two-volume biography entitled *A Complete Life of General George A. Custer*. It was the start of a relentless campaign fuelled by Whittaker to exonerate Custer of all blame at the Little Big Horn and to have Reno atone for his actions. Born in London, Whittaker was raised in Brooklyn when his parents emigrated to the United States in 1850.

He served in the 6th New York Cavalry during the Civil War, attaining the rank of brevet captain upon his discharge in August 1865. He took a teaching position for a whilst, but he did not derive much satisfaction from it. His passion was for writing and after an inheritance allowed him to marry, he purchased a house in Mount Vernon, New York, and settled down to explore his literary talent. His first attempts saw the sale of several articles and poems to various magazines and journals, later becoming a prolific writer of 'nickel and dime' fiction, otherwise known as 'penny dreadfuls', for Beadle and Adams, one of the leading publishers in this field. Although his short novels did produce a steady, if not respectable, income, they did not credit him with the fame of being a serious author that he clamoured for. During the Civil War, Whittaker had become an ardent admirer of George Custer, possibly because Custer was actually performing deeds of valour whereas Whittaker could only record them. Nevertheless, there is no doubt that Whittaker was deeply affected by the death of his hero and after writing a public eulogy to his beau sabreur, he began the research on his biography.

To obtain his first-hand information on Custer, Whittaker naturally turned to the widow, Elizabeth Custer, for help. Whether or not she actually provided the information he was seeking is not known for she always denied that she had, however, it is fairly obvious that much of the material contained in Whittaker's prodigious works would have been difficult to have been obtained from anywhere else. There is little doubt that Elizabeth Custer greatly influenced the writing of Edward S. Godfrey concerning her husband's final battle, so it can be safely assumed that she patronised Whittaker as well. Whittaker also drew heavily on Custer's own book *My Life on the Plains*; Civil War memoires and private letters plus interviews with some of the survivors of the battle. However, considering that he only took six months from the time of the battle to research, write, and get his work published, it is little wonder that his finished publication was flawed with numerous errors and misleading statements, and has remained a controversial biography to this day. Nevertheless, its glaring inaccuracies were glossed over and Elizabeth Custer wasted no time in heavily promoting the idyllic portrayal of her late husband that Whittaker had so skilfully written. Thus, the first full biography of George Armstrong Custer became an instant bestseller and Whittaker finally achieved his status as a serious writer, although it would not be the prestigious work that would carve his name in American history.

A widow at only 34 years old, Elizabeth Custer faced a formidable future. Like the wives of other army officers, she had always worried when George took to the field but he had never failed to return in the past and, as such, she had never really considered a life without him. This last campaign had proved to be difficult, he had failed to return and now she had to find a way to support herself. As if this was not enough, she also had the added responsibility of caring for her husband's elderly parents and her widowed sister in law. George's insurance of $4,750 would not support them for very long and her government pension as a military widow was only $50 per month, a fact highlighted by 'Frank Leslie's Illustrated Newspaper' dated 2nd May 1885, wherein it was reported that the pension had been recently doubled. She had no option but to return to the east, where her friends would rally round and support her. One even went so far as to ask government officials of President Grant to commission Elizabeth as the Postmistress of Monroe Post Office in Michigan. However, she could never find it within herself to forgive Grant for his distasteful condemnation of her husband or the fact that he had never even offered his condolences. On hearing of her friend's actions she categorically replied that she would,

> '… rather eat with hogs before she accepted any help from his administration!'

Be that as it may, Elizabeth had to find a means to survive and for a while she found employment by acting as secretary to the Society of Decorative Art, who were only too willing to have such a famous person within their circle. It was a propitious employment but it did not alleviate the agony that she silently endured. George, her beloved 'Autie' was dead and there were many who publicly blamed him for the disaster at the Little Big Horn. The former was a personal burden that she would have to bear for the rest of her life. The latter was an abhorrence she just could not tolerate. Then, she began her crusade to reinstate her husband's image and reputation; first by writing articles for newspapers and journals, then by making speeches at public engagements. She was determined to make George a revered martyr even though it was to be a time-consuming campaign that would continue until her death. Her ceaseless efforts drained her mentally and physically and there were many times when she felt she was not always as successful as she had hoped. On 13th May 1892, Elizabeth wrote in her journal:

> '... no one but myself knows how disappointed I am that I can do no better justice to 'Autie's' name...'

Elizabeth's articles had not gone unnoticed and literary friends, such as Henry James and Samuel Clemens, encouraged her to write her memoirs, particularly her life with George and his campaigns on the plains. She took their advice and although she enjoyed writing immensely, she found the research particularly painful. Her first book, *Boots and Saddles*, was published in 1885. Two years later, she published another book entitled, *Tenting on the Plains*, which was followed by her last book, *Following the Guidon*, in 1890. Whilst not being works of a literary genius, they are considered by many to be a fairly accurate account of Custer's military activities from the close of the Civil War until his untimely death and they served as superb propaganda in promoting her husband's memory. For future historians these books contain a wealth of information within the Custer legacy.

Legends are not born, they are created. George Armstrong Custer was already a Civil War hero when he took to the plains and it was through the tireless efforts of Elizabeth that he became a legend of the American West. An eloquent speaker, Elizabeth found herself in great demand as she toured the States, giving lectures at numerous functions and reading from her very popular books. What Frederick Whittaker had sown she would nurture into full bloom. Whittaker's biography of George had impressed her, particularly the denunciation of Marcus Reno, not to mention other officers of the Seventh who had survived the fight such as Benteen, whom she also believed had failed in their duty to go to her husband's aid. Whittaker had publicly accused Reno of cowardice, making him directly responsible for Custer's death and Elizabeth jumped at the providential opportunity to produce a scapegoat. If Reno was found to be guilty then her husband could be exonerated.

By 1878, sales of Whittaker's monumental biography had dwindled. Elizabeth had yet to publish her books and Whittaker sincerely wanted Custer's name to be cleared of any blemish. He had laid the foundations but it was not enough. Someone had to take the blame for the disaster at the Little Big Horn and Reno seemed the obvious choice. Whittaker became obsessed in his efforts to prove that Reno was to blame and, in all fairness, Reno had done very little in his own defence to purge the accusation. In fact, his actions during this period only added wood to the fire.

As senior officer in the field Reno had assumed temporary command of the regiment once the discovery of Custer's body had been made. It had been militarily correct to do so, although it had not been a popular act by any means. Lieutenant Godfrey for one, found Reno's harsh style of command offensive and he noted the fact in his journal:

> 'Reno's self-important rudeness makes him unbearable.'

A few others had also noted that Reno had begun drinking more heavily than usual since his return to the fort. This was not uncommon on the frontier where Indian attacks were frequently savage in their execution and the fort offered little else to do. Officers could afford the bitter liquor sold by the sutlers and more of it and although it did nothing to erase their memories, it did alleviate the stress to some extent. It was a practice that generally went unnoticed and it does seem rather unfair that Reno's partaking of the beverage has been so heavily documented, more so than anyone else.

Pressure on Reno was further increased when Confederate General Thomas Rosser publicly accused him of having abandoned Custer within a month or so of the battle. Reno, unwisely, took up the challenge and entered into a prejudicial correspondence with the general. Such communications did little to ease the tension that was building inside Reno, but it gave precious ammunition to Custer idolators, such as Whittaker. The first stone had been cast and others would follow at a rapid rate, all of them having Elizabeth Custer's stamp of approval.

Shortly after his return to Fort Abraham Lincoln, Reno clashed with a lieutenant of the 20th Infantry. The exact cause of their argument has never been fully established, although it would not be difficult to surmise. In any event, the fight was witnessed by other officers as the two men grappled on the floor of the officer's mess. Lieutenant Varnum attempted to intervene and Reno was none too pleased, even to the point of challenging Varnum to a duel. Eventually, Reno's anger subsided but he refused to shake Varnum's hand before storming out of the mess. Fellow officers had had enough and one even went so far as to press charges against Reno. Striking a subordinate officer was a serious offence, but the military hierarchy did not want to instigate court martial proceedings so soon after a devastating engagement with hostile Indians, particularly one that Reno had been heavily involved in and one in which Custer had died. Custer's demise was still making the front pages of the newspapers and a mess brawl would do nothing to enhance the reputation of the regiment. Therefore, the matter was dropped but the whole affair had left a bitter taste amongst the other officers at the fort and Reno was given a wide berth, a fact duly noted by his superiors.

In an effort to defuse the situation, Reno was posted to Fort Abercrombie in Dakota, where he was assigned as the post commander. Although he performed his duty quite adequately, his heavy drinking continued and he soon found himself entangled in a dubious relationship with the wife of a fellow Seventh Cavalry officer, Emily Bell. Her husband, Captain James Bell, had been temporarily assigned duties at another post and it was not the first time that Emily had taken advantage of her husband's absence. Captain Benteen later stated that Emily Bell,

> '...was a musky fox who was doubtless a nymphomaniac.'

From available records it is doubtful that Reno ever succeeded in his advances on Emily Bell, as she not only rebuffed him but was casting eyes in other directions. Reno, obviously hurt by Emily's rejection, is alleged to have implied:

> 'Mrs Bell's reputation is like a spoiled egg, you cannot hurt it.
> She is notorious in the regiment as a loose character.'

Whether or not Reno actually succeeded in having an affair with Emily Bell is a matter of conjecture. In all likelihood he probably didn't, but he had not been discreet and his advances had been witnessed by the serving officers at the fort, who duly reported Reno's actions to Captain Bell upon his return. In all probability, Bell was only too aware of his wife's improprieties during his absences, but being an 'officer and a gentleman' he had no other option but to protect her reputation and, if the truth were known, some of these very officers who had accused Reno of nefarious activities had, in fact, been willing partners of Emily Bell themselves. Bell wasted no time in instigating proceedings against Reno and the convening court martial found him guilty of 'conduct unbecoming of an officer and a gentleman'. It was a scandal that the regiment could ill afford and Reno was sentenced to be dismissed from the service. Although the findings of the court were upheld by the newly elected President Rutherford B. Hayes, he felt that in this instance the punishment did not fit the crime and he commuted the sentence to suspension from rank and pay for two years, commencing on 1st May 1877.

The actions of the military authorities during this phase of Reno's career are bizarre to say the least. Reno had committed a serious offence when he struck a subordinate officer, yet his superiors chose not to do anything.

Why? The affair over Emily Bell was a trivial matter, for it was not his actions but his verbal attack that landed him in trouble and yet again Reno escaped dismissal from the service. Why? Following Custer's death at the Little Big Horn, the public were demanding a scapegoat and Reno's actions certainly gave them one. If, as we can assume, Custer's death had been the result of an elaborate conspiracy, it is doubtful that the conspirators would have foreseen such a gift in Reno. However, for the present they chose not to use him, although any inquiry could be carefully orchestrated to work in their favour as well. Inquiries also have unknown elements. Were they afraid that a serious inquiry might expose them? Grant may not be president now, but he was still alive. Sheridan and Sherman had too much to lose as we shall see.

Captain James M. Bell is well documented within the military archives. He had joined the Seventh Cavalry as a second lieutenant in 1866 and for the next few years served admirably as the regimental quartermaster, being promoted to first lieutenant in 1867. He was absent, on leave, during the summer campaign of 1876, being recalled in July and promoted to captain as commanding officer of Company F to fulfil the vacancy being established on the death of Captain George Yates. Of Emily Bell there is nothing, not even a mention in Bell's biographies. Thus, it is impossible to reach a conclusion concerning her behaviour at Fort Abercrombie or anywhere else for that matter. Private journals seem to state she was a loose woman and, indeed, Reno was of that opinion. However, she was not shown to be so during the subsequent court hearing where Reno was found to be guilty. The truth may never be known, but it is a very grey shadowy area and the possibility cannot be ruled out that it was all a 'setup' with Emily as the bait.

Whittaker had obviously followed these events with mounting interest and he was becoming convinced that his allegations against Reno were founded. As the first year of Reno's suspension from duty drew to a close, Whittaker struck again and the bitter legacy of the Little Big Horn reared before a very demoralised Major Marcus Reno once more. On the 18th May 1878, Whittaker wrote to W.W. Corlett, a Congressman from Wyoming:

> 'Having been called upon to prepare the biography of the late Brevet Major General George A. Custer, USA, a great amount of evidence, oral and written, came into my hands, tending to prove that the sacrifice of his life and the lives of his immediate

> command at the Battle of the Little Big Horn was useless, and owing to the cowardice of his subordinates.
>
> I desire therefore, to call your attention, and that of Congress, through you, to the necessity of ordering an official investigation by a committee of your honourable body into the conduct of the United States troops engaged in the Battle of the Little Big Horn, fought on June 25th 1876, otherwise known as the Custer Massacre, in which Lieut. Col. Custer, Seventh United States Cavalry, perished with five companies of the Seventh Cavalry, at the hands of the Indians.'

This is an extraordinary request and one that neither Sheridan nor Sherman could allow. If Congress handled any inquiry, they would have no control over it. It was imperative that the army convened a court of inquiry that they could control. Whittaker's letter continues:

> 'The reasons on which I found my request are as follows:
>
> First: Information coming to me from participants in the battle, written and oral, is to the effect that gross cowardice was displayed therein by Major Marcus A. Reno, seventh United States cavalry, second in command; and that owing to such cowardice, the orders of Lieut. Col. Custer, commanding officer, to said Reno, to execute a certain attack, were not made.
>
> That the failure of this movement, owing to his cowardice and disobedience, caused the defeat of the United States forces on the day in question; and that had Custer's orders been obeyed, the troops would probably have defeated the Indians…'

Whittaker then goes on to describe the arrival of Captain Benteen,

> 'Whereupon, the Captain and his forces were placed under the command of Reno, who chose to remain idle despite the sound of gunfire being heard in the distance.'

He then asserts that his second exhibition of cowardice and incompetency resulted in the deaths of Custer and his men. Unfortunately, Whittaker does not name his informants, therefore his accusations must be regarded as conjectural. He continues;

> 'Second, the proof of these facts lies in the evidence of the United States Government, chiefly in the Army, and no power short of Congress can compel the attendance and protect them from annoyance and persecution if they openly testify to the cowardice exhibited on the above occasion.'

Just who is Whittaker referring to? Government officials and senior army officers were not at the battle or anywhere near it, thus any comments they may have are pure hearsay. If senior officers were to testify, why would they be open to persecution? Why does he not name them, if they have important information? The letter continues:

> 'Third: the only official record of the battle now extant is the report written by Major Reno, above named, and is, in the main, false and libellous to the memory of the late Lieut. Col. Custer, in that it represents the defeat of the United States forces on that occasion as owing to the division by Custer of his forces into three detachments, to overmanning his forces, and to the ignorance of the enemies forces, -all serious charges against the capacity of said Custer …'

Whittaker then counteracts this by putting the blame on Reno through his cowardice and disobedience. However, Captain Benteen has not escaped his wrath. He refers to the wilful neglect of Reno and Benteen to go to the aid of Custer, thus leaving him to his fate. Amongst other errors in Whittaker's letter, is the fact that he states the only report of the battle was written by Reno. Reno did write a report as he was required to do so, but then so did Benteen and many other officers who were present. Whittaker presses on:

> 'Fourth: The welfare of the United States Army demands that in the case of a massacre of a large party of troops, under circumstances covered with suspicion, it should be officially established where the blame belongs, to the end that the service may not deteriorate by the retention of cowards.'

That comment would be commonplace in any court of law, even today. It is unclear what Whittaker is trying to achieve, other than notoriety, if he does not produce named sources. He continues on:

> 'Fifth: Justice to an officer of previously unstained record of Lieut. Col. Custer, demands that the accusation under which his memory now rests, in the only official account of the Battle of the Little Big Horn now extant, should be proved or disproved...'

Whittaker is obviously not a man of few words, but his letter to Congressman Corlett is extremely interesting. Like his biography of Custer it is flawed with inaccuracies which probably became embedded during his hurried research and his obviously biased opinion of Custer has resulted in a clouded presumption. His research should have been more thorough than it actually was. His opening line is a misleading statement, which should have made Corlett suspicious of the contents of the letter as a whole, for Whittaker clearly states that he had 'been called upon to prepare a biography'. As far as records show, Whittaker had not been approached by anyone to complete the work and, as Elizabeth Custer had always denied any involvement in the project, to whom was Whittaker referring? His own self-opinionated ego perhaps?

In collating his information, Whittaker was clearly either not capable of interpreting the facts he had or he had no wish to do so. Thus, it appears that he probably included misleading statements in a deliberate attempt to condemn Reno before any official action could transpire, an act that was in itself libellous and one aimed at Benteen as well. Amongst the accusations of cowardice and disobeying orders, Whittaker also charges Reno with making 'false and libellous reports,' stating that Reno's report is the only official one filed. Then Whittaker compounds this mistake by stating that Custer's record is squeaky clean, which it most certainly was not! Custer had been court martialled twice during his career: in 1861 and again in 1867. Custer may have enjoyed a distinguished career but it was certainly not unblemished. With so many glaring inaccuracies, why was Whittaker's letter taken so seriously in government circles?

The answer to that question, in all probability, lay with Generals Sheridan and Sherman, who were very close friends of ex-President U. S. Grant and were now quite closely associated with the current president through their close relationship with Crook, who was a close friend and supporter of Rutherford B. Hayes. So, it all carries on, the circles becoming ever wider and complex. Friendship can be a very powerful tool in the world of politics, but it can also be a very deadly one and this has been evident since the dawn of civilisation. Only three men had their reasons for having Custer removed but only Sheridan and Sherman were in a position to achieve it without arousing suspicion and although the evidence to implicate them in a conspiracy is circumstantial and controversial, it is there and should be seriously considered.

Custer had already shaken a scandalous Grant administration; by forcing the resignation of the secretary of war and by implicating Grant's brother in various nefarious deals on the frontier. The result was to incur the wrath of the president which would be permanent. Custer has also severely criticised both Sheridan and Sherman, who must have taken it as personal insults. Encouraged by numerous newspaper magnates who wanted Custer to be a presidential candidate and who hung on every word he said, Custer had ensured that neither Sheridan nor Sherman would be suitable candidates for the nominations. In fact, the very idea that Custer could preside over them as a commander in chief was abhorrent to both of them. However, Custer was extremely popular and the likelihood of him becoming president was very real and they could not let that happen. It is not clear whether or not Custer saw himself as president, probably not for it was not his lifestyle, but the newspapers did and what they printed could produce votes in his favour without his even knowing about it. Sherman had further suffered from Custer's scathing remarks when he was severely censured by Custer concerning his harsh attitude towards the reconstruction of the South. Thus, neither Sheridan nor Sherman could see Custer as a favourable ally in the future and they must have harboured a growing resentment towards him. Custer was not just Grant's problem, he was theirs too. It could be that the friendship they shared with Grant was just a façade for their personal aspirations.

Grant had suspended Custer. It was the most he could do at the time. But that left Custer free to give interviews to journalists who clamoured for a scoop and Grant had no way of knowing what Custer might disclose next. If Custer was assigned to a remote post on the frontier, his very nature would induce him to write to his friends in the east and more revelations would most certainly appear in the newspapers. Without even knowing it Custer had signed his own death warrant and the conspiracy between Sheridan and Sherman blossomed.

Hostilities on the frontier and an impending campaign against the Indians provided the perfect scenario. The Seventh Cavalry were to participate in the campaign and Custer had to ride with them. Therefore, without disclosing their reasons, Sheridan and Sherman implored Grant to allow Custer to return to his regiment. Letters were carefully written so as not to arouse any suspicion and it is only by careful study of these documents that the subversive plans fall into place. The hostile Indians would do their dirty work and they would not even be aware of it. Custer's own panache in battle would determine that. The hard part would be getting the military machine to play their part, unaware of the conspiracy, whilst at the same time appearing to deal with the Indian question.

A cursory glance at the plans for the campaign will reveal that the military knew the area in which the hostiles could be found. Sheridan and Sherman also knew, albeit roughly, that a considerable number of hostile Indians had amassed and were ready to fight to the death for their freedom. Reports from the Indian agencies told them that. Much of this highly important information was not revealed to the field commanders and Sheridan had carefully drafted his orders to Crook and Terry so as not to betray their underlying purpose. Once Custer had been released into the field, Sheridan deftly instructed his commanders to delay further troop movements, thus leaving Custer out on his own. The surprise attack on Crook by the Rosebud had been a bonus. Crook obediently waited for reinforcements and supplies, much to the chagrin of his troops. Terry moved his troops 'cautiously' to the keen observer, but careful enough that he did not encounter any hostiles.

Following the Battle of the Little Big Horn, Sheridan had deliberately withheld Captain Poland's reports until he eventually dispatched the unlucky officer to a remote frontier post, where he could not continue to be a nuisance. The summer campaign of 1876 had been deliberately undermined to ensure that the military would not have a victory so close to Custer's death. He was a national hero and it did not matter how much the public still worshipped him, he was a dead hero. The hostiles would be held responsible for his death and, riding on a heavily orchestrated wave of public revulsion, they would be hunted down in a wake of revenge and the army would assume full responsibility for the deaths of these miscreants. But the timing had to be right. No one would even suspect that either Sheridan or Sherman could possibly be responsible for Custer's death. They were extremely clever in covering their conspiracy and they had no concerns regarding the repercussions of their actions that could result. Unless, that is, they began to lose control of the situation. But for the present it was the perfect murder.

Terry would never discuss the battle or anything concerning the campaign as a whole for the rest of his life. Of course it is possible that he may have realised that Sheridan's orders were not what they appeared to be and he had also been visibly shocked at the sight of Custer's remains on the battlefield. If this was the case, then he would be very careful not to reveal his concerns, save that he would never allow Custer to be blamed for the disaster. On 9th December 1876, Terry wrote to Sherman requesting that he make some correction to his annual report. He was obviously not happy with what Sherman had written, but his request was very tentative. Terry wrote:

> 'I see in your Annual Report you quote at length my dispatch from the Little Big Horn battlefield. That dispatch was so mangled by the telegraph, that in some places it is almost nonsense. In my Annual Report I give it as it was sent, and I respectfully request that the quotation in your report be corrected to correspond with the latter.'

Terry obviously felt that Sherman had misused his report for his own ends, but he would not openly say as much. For his part, Sherman would never have thought that any of his senior officers would have questioned his authority. After all he was the senior General of the Army.

Events following the battle had threatened to spiral out of control, as public indignation rose to fever pitch, but the furore had eventually run its course and appeared to calm down. Whittaker had enjoyed the profitable sales from his biography and Elizabeth Custer had continued to promote the martyrdom of her late husband, both of whom had been regarded as mere nuisances by Sheridan and Sherman. But they were a constant itch that would just not go away. Two years later, with sales of his biography now seriously declining, Whittaker was pushing for an inquiry into Reno's conduct and aided by a willing Elizabeth Custer, the battle was once again brought to the attention of the public. Sheridan and Sherman desperately needed a distraction that would end the affair once and for all. If the public needed a scapegoat, they would provide one and, as such, they were all in favour of an inquiry, especially one they could orchestrate and control through the military.

However, it was not Whittaker nor Elizabeth Custer that would provide the catalyst. It was Major Marcus A. Reno. Stunned by the overwhelming support for Whittaker's letter to Corlett, which had been the subject of newspaper coverage on 13th June 1878, Reno wrote to President Hayes eight days later:

> '... and I now respectfully appeal to the Executive for a "Court of Inquiry" to investigate the affair, that many rumours started by camp gossip may be set to rest and the truth made fully known...'

Whittaker had erroneously supplied the bait and Reno had snapped it up. Shunned by his fellow officers, widowed, and at a very low ebb in his life, Reno was the perfect scapegoat whether he was found to be guilty or not. Sheridan and Sherman could now breathe a sigh of relief. Official paperwork would cloud the system and time would conceal any evidence of their spurious involvement. What was more important, it would remain within the military where they could control the unfolding events.

Rutherford Birchard Hayes, another ex-general of the Civil War and a Republican from Ohio, granted Reno's request and directed Sherman to execute the order. Sherman duly complied, issuing special orders (Q.Q.979) No. 255 on 35th November 1878:

> '2. By direction of the President and on the application of Major Marcus A. Reno, 7th Cavalry, a Court of Inquiry is hereby appointed to assemble at Chicago, Illinois, on Monday the 13th day of January, 1879 or as soon thereafter as practicable for the purpose of inquiring into Major Reno's conduct at the battle of the Little Big Horn River on 25th and 26th days of June 1876. The Court will report the facts and its opinions as to whether from all the circumstances in the case, any further proceedings are necessary.'

The die had been cast and the Battle of the Little Big Horn was about to be re-enacted, but not perhaps as everyone had perceived it.

Chapter 5

Distant Drums

Much has been written in regard to Reno's lack of judicial response to the numerous libellous allegations that were hurled at him in the wake of the battle, including the inane accusations that he did not request a court of inquiry until the Statute of Limitations had run its course. In other words, until the statute was beyond the point where he could be tried by a court martial. The few occasions that Reno did respond by writing to the individual concerned, his correspondence inevitably became public knowledge through the newspapers and did not help his credibility. However, there is no evidence to explain Reno's reluctance to prove his innocence to the public at large or his accusers, and this still remains a grey area for historians.

The legal aspects of a court of inquiry are different from those of a court martial, although they are both subject to similar judicial legislation. In view of the notoriety and complexity of Reno's case, it may be advisable to summarise the duties and responsibilities of a court of inquiry as opposed to a court martial.

The purpose of a court of inquiry is to investigate all the facts concerning a person's actions during a military operation, with the view of determining the truth and to report their findings to the convening authority. Unlike a court martial, it does not pass any judgement or sentence accordingly, for it is not required to express opinions or make any further recommendations, unless it has been specifically requested to do so. A court of inquiry is usually presided over by three senior serving officers and both the convening authority and the defence can employ their own lawyers to present the case. During the proceedings witnesses can be summoned to testify and subsequently be subject to examination from both sides. Thus, the duties of the officers engaged in a court of inquiry appear to be similar to those of a court martial or even a civil court, to determine the truth but that is all.

When Reno did officially request a court of enquiry, he did so within the two years as required by the Statute of Limitations, but only just. He could not at any time request a court martial and would have had no reasons to do so. Such a course of action was out of the question anyway. The military authorities had no reason to convene a court martial as no charges had been officially filed against him concerning his conduct at the Little Big Horn. Whittaker could not demand any official proceedings against Reno, although given the chance there is no doubt he would have done so. Whittaker was neither employed by the military nor was he a participant in the battle, so his so-called 'evidence' was nothing more than hearsay. As such, Whittaker could not produce any positive proof of his libellous allegations against Reno, or Benteen for that matter. However, he was subpoenaed to attend the inquiry and invited to disclose the names of those who had provided him with information, although he was strictly forbidden to take any active part in the proceedings himself.

Examining the transcript of the 'Reno Court of Inquiry', as it became known, is an onerous task and should not be undertaken lightly. This probably explains why little has been published on it. The eminent historian, Lieutenant Colonel William A Graham who became a recognised authority on the battle, was the first researcher to realise the potential the court records could disclose. Following the First World War, Graham was attached to the judge advocate general's corps, where the original transcript of the inquiry had been kept, undisturbed for over forty years. His search proved fruitful and after he had copied the lengthy documents, he had positive material to enhance the books he subsequently wrote and which still remain the main source of information for modern historians.

The inquiry took twenty-six days to complete and the original transcript is approximately 1,300 pages in length, including the numerous maps and letters that were submitted as evidence. It is interesting reading and, contrary to popular belief, it was not a 'military whitewash', at least not in the sense that some writers would have us believe. Under the circumstances that prevailed at that time, it was not only a sensible course to take but the right one.

In accordance with protocol, Reno had been granted an inquiry by the president, however, his request had not been granted for purely military reasons nor for the fact that he had requested one. Rutherford B. Hayes had his own political motives for allowing an inquiry to take place. His predecessor, Grant, had retired from the position not wishing to seek another term. He had suffered the ignominy of his administration being raked by one scandal after another. Domestic factions within the political circles had seized every opportunity to crack the Republican nut and it is not unreasonable to assume that George Custer had been manipulated in such a manner when he gave his evidence against Belknap and Orville Grant. It is also not unreasonable to suggest that as Custer was already a national hero, Democratic fanatics envisaged Custer as a future president and with the backing of their unlimited finances there is every justification to assume they felt Custer would win. Opinion as to whether Custer aspired to such ambitious heights is divided, although it is doubtful whether Custer would actually give up his exciting and varied life on the plains for a paper job in an office. In any event, the Democratic dreams had been shattered by Custer's demise and they blamed Grant for their loss. The Democrats clamoured for an inquiry, endorsing the actions of notables such as Whittaker and Elizabeth Custer.

Hayes was a Republican like Grant and on accepting the Presidency he, unfortunately, inherited the stigma of the previous administration. It was an anathema he was eager to extricate himself from. Hayes' election as president was not without its own drama and controversy. His apposite in the 1876 election had been Samuel J. Tilden, a Democrat from New York. Tilden had actually won more popular votes than Hayes, who hovered on the brink of defeat, but then the returns from several states came under dispute and Hayes' future hung in the balance. A Republican nominated Congressional Electoral Committee investigated the dispute and subsequently awarded all the questionable votes to Hayes, which secured him a majority of one in the Electoral College. Not a very auspicious start to his administration, not to mention a questionable one.

The new president made very few changes within his government and the military still retained Sherman as its commander. Hayes had been a major general during the Civil War and it can be safely presumed he was on friendly terms with Sherman and recognised his capabilities. However, at the same time the new president had to be seen by his adversaries, if not the general populace, to be making an effort to sweep away the lingering cobwebs that threatened to mar his Republican policies. The Reno Court of Inquiry would be a start in the right direction, for if nothing else it would quell the persistent discontent within the Democratic faction for a while. The result of the Inquiry was immaterial, whether Reno was found guilty or not was of little consequence. What mattered was that Hayes had to be seen doing the right thing by all concerned. It would herald the new reforms he had prepared for the future.

As General of the Army and therefore the convening authority, Sherman could carefully orchestrate the court of inquiry fight from the start. He had to prove that the army had nothing to hide and to that end the Inquiry would serve as a very useful tool. As if to emphasize that point, Sherman included in the Special Orders No. 255 of November 1878:

> 'The Court will report the facts and its opinions as to whether from all the circumstances in the case, any further proceedings are necessary.'

Sherman also added that the departmental commanders should set the date of the inquiry and that it should, if possible, be held at Fort Abraham Lincoln in Dakota Territory, where the majority of the witnesses would be available. Apart from the fact that Sherman had failed to check whether or not such witnesses were available in one location, which they were not, such a recommendation was not included in the Special Orders No. 255, which clearly stated that the inquiry would be held in Chicago and would convene on 13 January the following year. Thus, it appears that his directive to the department commanders was purely conciliatory.

The commanding general of the department of Dakota was none other than General Alfred Terry, who had no desire to be part of the proceedings anyway. At the time he received his orders from Adjutant General Townsend, he was visiting the military academy at West Point and he dutifully replied that he would comply as soon as the current military operations were over, thus ensuring the availability of the witnesses required. Here, controversy arises yet again, for it appears from available sources that Terry's involvement in the Reno Court of Inquiry ended with Townsend's missive. As the commander of the Dakota Territory, he had merely been accorded the courtesy of notification.

It must be remembered that the judicial system within the military was in its infancy at this time. It was nowhere near as precise or sophisticated as it is today. It was much easier then, to manipulate the proceedings and destroy any incriminating evidence. To do that successfully, the presiding officers had to be chosen carefully and, here again, Sherman had to rely on Sheridan to make the selection. News of the impending inquiry had already found its way into various newspapers and journals, some of which viewed the inquiry with scepticism. 'The Army and Navy Review' of November 1878 solemnly declared:

> 'We trust that this investigation will be complete and decisive.'

Sheridan chose wisely. The officers serving under Terry were out of the question as the majority of them had been too closely involved in the ill-fated campaign, added to which Terry had already questioned his superior's doctrine. Sheridan therefore looked at the officers serving in Crook's command. It was no secret throughout the service, that Crook had disliked Custer since that day in 1865 when he had got into difficulties at Sayler's Creek and Custer had extricated him from a near disaster. It had been a humiliating incident and Crook could bear a grudge for a very long time. Perhaps this dislike had been foremost in Sheridan's mind when Crook had been assigned to the Army of the Platte for the 1876 campaign. There was no doubt that Crook had served them well up to now, whether the general was aware of that fact or not and he would probably continue to do so. In all probability, Crook would have assisted Sheridan in making the final selection: Colonel John H. King, Colonel Wesley Merritt, and Lieutenant Colonel W.B. Royall.

Colonel John Haskell King, the commanding officer of the 9th U.S. Infantry, had entered the army in 1838 having been appointed a second lieutenant in the 1st U.S. Infantry. The following year he had attained the rank of first lieutenant and by 1846 he had been promoted to captain. During his career, King had seen action in Florida against the Seminole Indians; at Vera Cruz in the Mexican War; and in Texas where he was stationed at the outbreak of the Civil War. Throughout the Civil War he had served with Union troops at Shiloh, Corinth, and Murfreesboro, being awarded brevet major general in 1865 for his services. In December 1866 King took command of the 9th U.S. Infantry, an appointment he held until his retirement in 1882. Companies C, G, and H of the 9th Infantry had been assigned to Crook's column in 1876 and saw action at the Battle of the Rosebud and Slim Buttes.

Colonel (George) Wesley Merritt, the commanding officer of the 5th U.S. Cavalry, was commissioned a second lieutenant following his graduation from the military academy at West Point in 1860. Thrust into the Civil War, he had served gallantly in the Union cavalry, being promoted to captain within two years of his service. His courage and determination in the field soon earned him recognition and following the Battle of Brandy Station in 1863, Merritt was appointed brigadier general of volunteers. Such a huge jump in rank was unusual, even for the Civil War which produced many surprises throughout its duration, but Wesley Merritt was by no means unique. There were others who were also rewarded for their panache on the field of battle, one of which had been George Armstrong Custer. Merritt had served alongside Custer in the Army of the Potomac and the two cavalrymen became firm friends, with Merritt later being a frequent visitor of the Custers at their headquarters on the plains. As such Elizabeth Custer must have been delighted when she heard that he would be one of the presiding officers at the inquiry. In 1866 he was assigned as lieutenant colonel of the 9th U.S. Cavalry and was instrumental in assisting to subdue several Indian uprisings. By 1876, having received his colonelcy and taken command of the 5th U.S. Cavalry, Merritt had another brush with hostile Indians at Warbonnet Creek whilst marching to join Crook's column in July. Merritt was a highly respected serving officer and he was probably chosen because of his long-standing relationship with Custer, of whom it was felt that he had an intimate knowledge. Merritt made no secret of the fact that he disliked Reno, but being a professional soldier he did not allow his personal feelings to cloud his judgement.

Lieutenant Colonel William Bedford Royall, of the 3rd U.S. Cavalry, had also served in the Mexican War and had had his first taste of Indian warfare in a skirmish with Comanche Indians at Coon Creek in 1848. Stationed in Texas he had more than one brush with the Comanche over the next few years, before being promoted to captain at the onset of the Civil War. Whether or not he had become acquainted with King during his four years of duty in the Mexican War or in Texas is not known, but it is a possibility. Royall's regiment was attached to the Army of the Potomac, where he may have encountered George Custer or Wesley Merritt, although there is no evidence to suggest that he did. He was severely wounded by sabre cuts at Old Church, which disabled him for some time, forcing him to serve the remainder of the Civil War recruiting for the army. In 1868, Royall found himself in the field fighting hostile Indians in Kansas. Custer was also engaged in the Indian conflicts in Kansas during 1868 and Royall could possibly have made Custer's acquaintance then, although there is no record of the fact. He was promoted to lieutenant colonel of the 3rd U.S. Cavalry in December 1875, and the following year was in command of Crook's cavalry at the Battle of the Rosebud. Royall was also present when Crook's forces joined Terry's command in August, where he may have encountered Reno. There is no evidence to suggest that the two officers engaged in conversation, but the fact that they had both had a traumatic experience with the hostile Sioux and Cheyenne, and given that curiosity forms a large part of human nature, it would not seem unreasonable to suggest that they did enjoy an exchange of experiences. Even if they didn't, Royall would have been fully aware of the rumours that were circling concerning Reno's conduct at the Little Big Horn.

Given the vast publicity that Custer's death had generated, it may not have been easy to select totally independent adjudicators for the inquiry.

However, even a cursory glance at the officers who had been chosen shows that they may have had their own private interests in the investigation. They were all well acquainted with each other, even if they were not intimately friendly, for they all served with or under Crook. Merritt had been a very close friend of Custer and had made no attempt to hide his dislike for Reno. Sheridan could have looked at other officers, for example in the east, but it would have proven difficult to assess their qualities to take part in his deadly game and still retain control. Crook had carefully chosen the officers whom he knew would perform accordingly; Sheridan had approved of the selection; and, Sherman could keep a tight grip on the reins. If the court of inquiry had been an unforeseen event, the situation was evolving perfectly.

The recorder for the court, who also served as the lawyer on behalf of the convening authority, was First Lieutenant Jesse M. Lee, adjutant of the 9th U.S. Infantry. By his own admission he was not an able lawyer and a more adroit member of the legal profession may have been able to extract more valuable testimony from the witnesses. (That is probably why he was chosen. Sheridan and Sherman did not want the truth to emerge, so Lee did his job admirably.) In any event it is evident throughout the original transcript of the proceedings that Lee did strive to fulfil his duty to the best of his ability, although whether he did manage to reveal the truth is a matter of conjecture. There is very little source material on Jesse M. Lee, however the noted historian W.J. Ghent wrote that the recorder of the court had written a letter some years after the inquiry stating:

> '… the Court has been imposed upon and my own opinions were completely altered.'

At the end of the day Lee knew the inquiry had been orchestrated and he was not impressed.

Reno, on the other hand, had employed the services of a professional lawyer to represent his case. Mr Lyman D. Gilbert of Harrisburg, Deputy Attorney General of Pennsylvania no less. A graduate of Yale Collage in 1865, Gilbert was admitted to the bar in 1868 and appointed Deputy Attorney General in 1873. He was small in both height and build, but he was impressive in a courtroom and given that military law was distinctly different from civil law, he was probably on a fairly even keel with Recorder Lee. Reno was obviously fully prepared to meet salvo with salvo and Lyman D. Gilbert was the perfect lawyer to do just that.

In accordance with the authority vested in him, Lee employed Mr H.C. Hollister as the official stenographer for the duration of the court. As a stenographer, Hollister left much to be desired. He made numerous serious blunders throughout the hearing that can clearly be observed in the original transcript. Unfortunately, his mistakes were not confined to the official records. The *Chicago Tribune* followed the unfolding drama with notable interest, printing the latest revelations on a daily basis and it is obvious that they must have had some sort of access to Hollister's court record for their prime source. On the opening day of the inquiry the court had previously decided that,

> '... it will sit with open doors, but further decides that no record or notes of the proceedings shall be taken for publication.'

Thus, newspaper reporters could observe but not record. They probably did take notes of course, but the articles that appeared in the *Chicago Tribune* also contained the errors that Hollister had made and if the information was not obtained directly from the court stenographer, then where did it originate? Sadly, very few copies of these editions of the *Chicago Tribune* have survived and those that have are extremely difficult to access.

Events, incidents and, in particular, disasters have always attracted an excess of conflicting rumours and the Reno Court of Inquiry was no exception. If Custer's defeat had caused a tremendous sensation, then the Reno Court of Inquiry would open old wounds to the sound of distant drums. The disaster was in the spotlight once more and with the populace clamouring for more information, if not a scapegoat, arguments were numerous and fights broke out in the streets. Unsubstantiated rumours do not quell arguments, they provoke them and one such rumour that circulated cast serious doubts on the integrity concerning some of the officers of the Seventh who testified at the inquiry, even going so far as to suggest that they may have committed perjury.

In an article published in 1936, W.J. Ghent wrote that a fellow researcher of the battle had been told by an unnamed officer of the Seventh, that the witness testimonies had been agreed upon before the court had convened. This unnamed officer stated:

> '...that the officers meeting in Reno's room at the Palmer House, drinking the Major's whiskey and smoking the Major's cigars, made a compact as to how they would testify.'

The article also claimed that Captain Godfrey had dismissed the rumour as a fabrication, adding,

> '... he had never heard of the compact.'

However, Godfrey then continues,

> '... he had repeatedly refused to go to Reno's room.'

It appears that Godfrey is being deliberately evasive, for collectively he refutes the rumour and then confirms it. His statement may not be conducive in dispelling the rumour, but it does portray an honourable disposition towards preserving the integrity of the officer class.

In addition, the same article refers to the recorder of the court, Lee who, in summing up, implied that an esprit de corps existed amongst the officers who had lately testified.

When examining the article it must be borne in mind that it is a piece of journalism and if Recorder Lee had made that implication, it may be due to the fact that he had been aware of the rumour. In actual fact, the rumour can be instantly discounted for, on the opening day of the proceedings Lee quite categorically stated that only two of his witnesses had arrived to testify. Who those witnesses were was not disclosed, but two officers hardly qualify for the basis of the rumour.

That Reno had a room in the Palmer House was common knowledge, after all it was a hotel and, if the truth be known, most if not all of the officers involved in the inquiry did as well. One room had even been engaged to serve as the courtroom. Reno may have unwisely entertained a few officers of the Seventh during the hearing and, quite probably had laid on whiskey and cigars as a host would, but in view of his social standing within military circles such gatherings were probably no more than simple reunions with a few old friends. To suggest that any of the officers of the Seventh had entered into a esprit de corps is broadening the rumour beyond credibility. The honour of the Seventh was never in doubt.

If Reno did entertain a few friends in his hotel room such an act did not contravene any legal issues. Reno was not on trial. He had not been officially charged with any misconduct or crime concerning his actions at the Little Big Horn. He had requested the court of inquiry in the face of public accusations of 'cowardice in the face of the enemy', predominantly levelled at him by Frederick Whittaker. The sole purpose of the inquiry was to establish the facts concerning the battle and to ascertain whether or not any official charges should be brought against the major. He had withstood a barrage of accusations for over eighteen months and now he would have his say, but in an official court. However, Reno knew that it was going to be an expensive venture. He had engaged a prominent lawyer and the Palmer Hotel was not cheap either. Having received no salary for over a year, his finances were not exactly robust. Lyman Gilbert had also been engaged to act as a financial guardian for his son Ross and Reno had borrowed $800 from his son's inheritance to offset his expenses, trading his life insurance policy as collateral. It was a risk Reno had to take. Thus, with finances at a premium it is unlikely that he hosted any lavish entertainment in his room, besides a glass of whiskey and a cigar.

As for the officers concerned, any attempt to manipulate their testimonies would have been a complete waste of time. Reno had very few admirers, especially within the Seventh, and even before Custer's death these officers had been divided in their loyalties. Therefore, those who testified at the hearing would either have been pro-Custer like Godfrey undoubtedly was, or anti-Custer such as Benteen, who made no attempt to conceal the fact. The inquiry would reinstate these factors and it is doubtful that either faction would look favourably upon Reno, in fact their testimonies reveal that they were quite non-committal. This division seems to defy time and endeavours to continue today with some historians openly displaying their views. Many authors are so pro-Custer that they will strongly defend him to their last breath, whilst those that condemn him often tend to support Reno. The fact is that both Custer and Reno had performed their duty to the utmost of their ability and neither of them should be held responsible for the disaster that had befallen them. Serious historians should view the events objectively and not fall into the trap just because it had always been so. Equally, rumours should be examined carefully and as most rumours have no evidence to support them, they should be viewed as speculation or uncorroborated hearsay.

Very little has been written concerning the venue of the court of inquiry: viz, the Palmer House in Chicago. From available sources it appears that this particular hotel was the third building of that name to have been built in Chicago by 1879. The first Palmer House stood on the corner of State and Quincy streets and had been erected in 1851. The second building, known generally as 'the Palmer' had been constructed by Potter Palmer on the southeast corner of State and Quincy streets and he had given it to his bride, Bertha Honore, as a wedding gift. The hotel opened its doors on

26th September 1871 and survived just thirteen days before it was razed to the ground in the Great Fire of Chicago. Undaunted, Palmer secured a loan for $1.7 million and immediately began the construction of another Palmer House, which was completed in 1873. In the wake of the Great Fire, the new building had been constructed primarily of brick and iron, thus giving rise to their advertisements that presumptuously declared the Palmer House to be,

> '... the world's only fire-proof hotel!'

The building itself was magnificently grandiose and intensely imposing. All the rooms were large and sumptuously decorated. Even the in-house barber shop was reputed to have a floor that had been inlaid with silver dollars. It was luxury on a very grand scale and, not unnatural for the times, was an instant success. Anyone and everyone stayed at the Palmer House when visiting Chicago, from politicians such as Ulysses S. Grant and William McKinley, to famous authors such as Charles Dickens and Oscar Wilde. Rudyard Kipling was not impressed by the exquisite grandeur at all and thought the whole place was extravagantly distasteful:

> '... A gilded and mirrored rabbit–warren and there I found a huge hall of tessellated marble.'

Thus, surrounded by unadulterated splendour and already clouded in speculation, the court of inquiry convened at eleven o'clock on Monday 13th January 1879 and the officiating members of the court were duly sworn in. However, it is apparent from the official transcript that neither side was fully prepared to enter into the proceedings by this date and considering the fact that they were engaging in an official military inquiry, concerning issues of potential gravity, those involved appear to have been extremely lax about the whole affair.

Recorder Lee calmly informed the presiding officers that not only had the majority of his witnesses failed to arrive but that he had only just received the documents he had requested from the War Department and, therefore, had not had the desired time to examine them in preparation for the hearing. Obviously, Lee could not control the arrival of the witnesses, but in view of the fact that seven weeks had elapsed since the date of Sherman's directive to the date of commencement of the inquiry and given the fact that officials in government positions are excruciatingly slow in dealing with internal issues, this still appears to be a very long delay in ensuring the appropriate documents were safely delivered to the court to give enough time to examine them. Such delay is suspect in judicial circles and rightly or wrongly leads the researcher to wonder whether or not these documents had been deliberately delayed on account of the nature of the investigation. Delays were common practice during a court martial where the defendant's future hung precariously in the balance. But this was not a life-or-death situation. The 'Articles of War' that governed all military court sessions had originally been established in 1806, during an era in which cases such as Reno's would not even have been contemplated. These early rules and regulations were not only ambiguous, tenuous, and severely outdated, they were the basis on which the court of inquiry was guided and would not be subject to reform until the latter part of the 1880s. It can be safely assumed that Sherman would have been fully conversant with these judicious laws and even if he was not, he had numerous aides who were. Even in its obsolete form it is not inconceivable that he would have taken advantage of the system. Thus, the documents that Lee finally received would probably have been thoroughly checked to ensure that the lieutenant only had access to the information that Sherman would have considered appropriate. Anything that did not meet the general's approval would have been quickly removed or even destroyed.

If Lee had his problems, then so did Reno, who had the embarrassing task of informing the court that his lawyer, Lyman Gilbert, had failed to arrive for the opening phase. The failure of witnesses to arrive on time was one thing, but the failure of a lawyer was another. Assuming that Gilbert was in possession of all their documentation, it would have been extremely difficult for Reno to enter into the proceedings on his own. Faced with these awkward situations the presiding officers had no alternative but to adjourn the inquiry until the following day and hope they could begin in earnest. The first day of the inquiry had lasted approximately one hour.

By the time the court reconvened the next day, Gilbert had arrived to represent Reno and having been accepted by the court, he entered into a lengthy discussion with Lee to determine the precise legal aspects of the inquiry that his client would be required to produce evidence for. The argument took up the remaining hours of the morning, with both Gilbert and Lee determined to stand their ground. Eventually, after the presiding officers had deliberated on the points raised, it was decided that the prime objective of the court was to determine Reno's conduct throughout the two days of the battle and to ascertain whether or not the decisions he made during that time had contributed in any way to the death of Custer and his battalion. It was an answer that had already been envisaged by Gilbert, but he was satisfied that it was now officially on record. He did not object to Lee being the first to call and examine witnesses.

The first officer to testify was First Lieutenant Edward Maguire, who had accompanied General Terry as chief engineer officer. Terry's column had arrived in the battle area on the 27th June, when the conflict had ended. As an engineer, Maguire had examined the battlefield with his Sergeant and prepared a report, to which he had attached a map as an exhibit for the court and referred to it extensively throughout the examination, during which it was revealed that Maguire's sergeant had collected the data and prepared the map. Maguire's testimony is, for the most part, contradictory and vague. He admitted that the map was inaccurate in many respects and when cross-examined by Gilbert as to the authenticity of his evidence, Maguire replied,

> 'Yes sir, it is hearsay evidence.'

In relation to future research, Maguire's testimony was a complete waste of time and he was not recalled at a later date.

Maguire was not the only witness to be called who could not enlighten the court with any specific evidence that related to Reno. In fact Lee appeared to dwell on the terrain, its flora, and relative distances in many of his examinations. Colonel John Gibbon, commander of the Montana column, also arrived in the area with Terry once the fighting had ended. He could only offer his observations of Reno's positions in the timber and on the bluff. He said that in his opinion neither areas were practicable in terms of defence, although he did not offer any alternative that Reno could have chosen. Gibbon had experience in campaigning against hostile Indians and he would have appreciated the problem that Reno had faced, although this was never mentioned during his short testimony. The few articles that he later wrote on the 1876 campaign are often overlooked by researchers, even though they contain a wealth of information. His writing shows an acute understanding of the army and the Indians at that time. In October 1877, Gibbon wrote an article for *The American Catholic Quarterly Review* in which he stated:

> 'You cannot point to one single treaty made with the Indians which has not at some time or other been violated by the

> whites, and you can point to innumerable instances where the Indian has been most outrageously swindled by the agents of the government; and the great wonder is, not that we have had so many wars but that we have had so few.'

It is a pity that Gibbon had not supported Custer when he had said the same thing not two years previously.

Incredibly, a further two witnesses were called to give evidence and neither of them were even in the vicinity of the battle! Lieutenant Colonel Michael V. Sheridan, who had held the rank of captain, was the commanding officer of Company L, 7th Cavalry in 1876. At the time of the battle he was on detached duty as military secretary to his brother, General Phil Sheridan, in Chicago. A very convenient appointment at the time, for it shows that Sheridan did not want the risk of allowing his brother to be involved in the 1876 campaign, after all he could be killed! Sheridan's testimony was also short and revealed nothing of note to the inquiry either. He confirmed that he had not actually visited the battlefield until July 1877 and then only to remove the bodies of the officers who had been killed. Sheridan produced a sketch, drawn by Captain Henry J. Nowlan of the Seventh, which showed where the named bodies of the officers had been found. Lee accepted the sketch as another exhibit, even though it had nothing to do with the issues brought before the court.

Captain R.S. Payne of the 5th U.S. Cavalry was the eighth witness to be called by Lee to testify. He was also a complete waste of time. He had not seen the battlefield until August 1878 and could only offer his opinion in respect to the defence positions of Custer's forces as suggested by the artefacts they had found in the area. The disposition of Custer's battalion would have been unknown to Reno at the time of the battle. Why these four officers had been summoned to give evidence is beyond reason. None of them had participated in the battle and, therefore, could not elucidate on the events or Reno's conduct at that time. Of course, it is conceivable that Sherman had put them on the list to either waste time or muddy the waters.

Four witnesses who had been with the pack train were examined; two officers of the Seventh and two civilian packers. Reno and his troops had been occupying the bluff for roughly an hour before the arrival of the pack train, indeed, Reno had even dispatched Second Lieutenant Hare to locate it and hurry it along. Therefore, none of these witnesses could testify as to Reno's conduct in the valley fight, but they could give their opinion concerning his actions on the bluff. When asked about Reno's conduct on their arrival, Captain Thomas McDougall, who had commanded Company B as escort to the pack train, replied that he thought the major seemed perfectly cool and although he could not observe any enthusiasm, Reno was as brave as any man there. First Lieutenant Edward Mathey, the officer who had commanded the pack train, was a little contradictory in his testimony and thought that Reno appeared excited when he arrived on the bluff, stating,

> '… When Major Reno came up to me, he was somewhat excited, as any man would be under the circumstances. It was not long since he came out of the fight and that would be a natural condition for a man to be in. I did not question his courage and saw no act to indicate lack of courage, or cowardice.'

These testimonies may appear inconsistent and vague but it must be remembered that they had arrived on the bluff whilst the fight was still raging around them, therefore their minds would have been occupied by more immediate duties than observing Reno's disposition. However, neither of these witnesses question Reno's courage at that time.

Civilian packer B.F. Churchill said that when he arrived with the pack train he could see men, mounted and on foot, still climbing up the bluff. Given the time lapse between Reno's retreat and Churchill's arrival, this seems very doubtful. He also testified that during the evening of the 25th June, he witnessed a confrontation between Reno and another civilian packer, John Frett, whom he referred to as 'Fritz'. Churchill stated that although he did not see Reno staggering or hear him stammering, he believed that the major did appear under the influence of alcohol. He added that he did see Reno make movements as if to strike Frett, but did not actually see him do so. Frett, on the other hand, claimed under oath that Reno did physically assault him that evening and that the officer did appear to be drunk. Frett then determined to question Captain Benteen's actions during the defence of the bluff by asserting that Benteen did not go anywhere near the mule packs to drive off skulkers, but he failed to mention that he had been caught there himself on several occasions. Benteen firmly contended that he had driven off skulkers from the mule lines on many occasions during the 25th and 26th June. For his part, Reno later testified that he did have a flask containing whiskey in his coat pocket. He also confirmed that he had had to chase the same packers out of the mule lines on many occasions and

General William T. Sherman 1820-1891.
General of the Army and a close friend of President Grant and Lt. General Phil Sheridan. A hard commander and not a man to cross. *(Photo: Mathew Brady. Kind Courtesy of the Still Pictures Section, Special Media Archive Services Division, National Archives. Now in Public Domain)*

Lt. General Philip Sheridan 1831-1888.
General Commanding the Department of the Missouri. He had no love for any Native American but was not adverse to using them to do his dirty work. *(Photo: Mathew Brady c.1880. Kind courtesy of the Library of Congress. Now in Public Domain)*

General Alfred Terry 1827-1890.
General Commanding the Dakota Column, of which the 7th Cavalry was a part. Following the battle at the little Big Horn he would never discuss either Custer or the defeat. *(Kind courtesy of Brady-Hardy photographic collection (Prints & Photo Division) Library of Congress. Now in Public Domain)*

Colonel John Gibbon 1827-1896.
Officer Commanding the Montana Column, later Commanding the Department of the Dakota. His troops joined Terry's Column on the march to the Little Big Horn. *(Photo: c. Civil War. Compiled by H.D. Milhollen & D.H. Mugridge, Washington D.C. Kind courtesy of the Library of Congress. Now in Public Domain)*

Lt. Colonel George A. Custer 1839-1876.
Titular Commanding Officer 7th Cavalry at the Little Big Horn. The public adored him, but his superiors feared him. Did that fear lead to conspiracy to murder? *(Photo: Mathew Brady. C. Civil War. Kind courtesy of the Prints and Photographs Division, Library of Congress. Now in Public Domain)*

Major Marcus A. Reno 1834-1889.
Second in Command 7th Cavalry. Reno was publically made a scapegoat for the defeat at the Little Big Horn which lead to his request for an inquiry to clear his name. *(Photo: D.F. Barry. Kind courtesy of Denver Public Library Special Collections. Now in Public Domain)*

***Above*: The Far West.**
A steamship on the Yellowstone & Missouri Rivers. Captain Grant March tool the wounded from the battle down to Bismarck and Fort A. Lincoln, breaking all records on the rivers. *(Photo: D. F. Barry. C. 1880. Kind courtesy of the Denver Public Library. Now in Public Domain)*

***Right*: Red Horse 1822-1907.**
A Miniconjou Sioux participant of the battle at the Little Big Horn. He drew 42 pictographs depicting the battle in an agency ledger. *(Photo: Originally published by D.F. Barry, although there is no evidence to state he was the photographer. Now in Public Domain)*

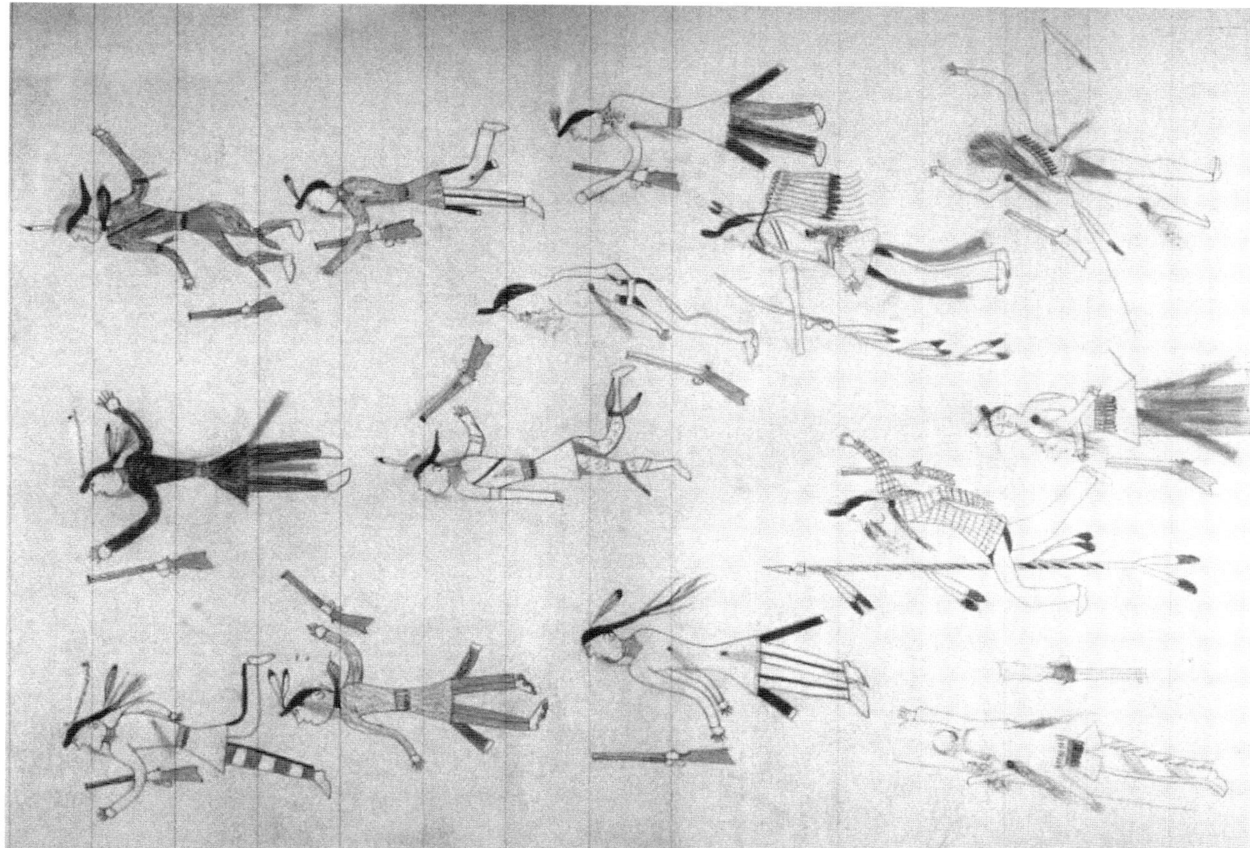

A pictographic account of the battle drawn by Red Horse.
1 of 42 that Red Horse drew of the battle in the Cheyenne River Agency Ledger book. *(Kind courtesy of the National Anthropological Archive, Smithsonian Institue. Manuscript 2367A. Now in Public Domain)*

A Cheyenne Pictograph c. 1878.
Another depiction of the battle, painted by an unknown Cheyenne artist on a bison hide. *(Kind courtesy of the Museum of the American Indian. Now in Public Domain)*

Keogh Memorial at the Little Big Horn Battlefield.
The original memorial to Captain Myles w. Keogh, erected on the site where he fell during the battle. The photograph was taken in 1879, with Captain G. Sanderson in the foreground, commanding officer of the burial detail. *(Photo; Stanley J. Morrow. Courtesy of the Montana Historical Society. Now in Public Doman)*

Crow Scouts at the Little Big Horn in 1913.
Former Army Scouts who rode with Custer to the battle. (Left to right) White-Man-Runs-Him, Hairy Mocassin, Curley and Goes Ahead. *(Kind courtesy of the U.S. Army. Now in Public Domain)*

Palmer House, Chicago.
The magnificent hotel where the Court of Inquiry was convened in January 1879. *(Kind courtesy of the Palmer House, a Hilton Hotel)*

Colonel John H. King 1818-1888.
Commanding Officer 9th U.S. Infantry Senior officer presiding at the Reno Court of Inquiry.
(Photo: c. ACW. Kind courtesy Prints & Photographic Division. Library of Congress. Now in Public Domain)

Colonel Wesley Merritt 1836-1810.
Commanding Officer 5th U.S. Cavalry Presiding officer at the Reno Court of Inquiry. Merritt was a former Commanding Officer to Major Reno, later serving at Slim Buttes under General G. Crook. *(Photo: c. ACW. Kind courtesy of Prints & Photographic Division, Library of Congress. Now in Public Domain)*

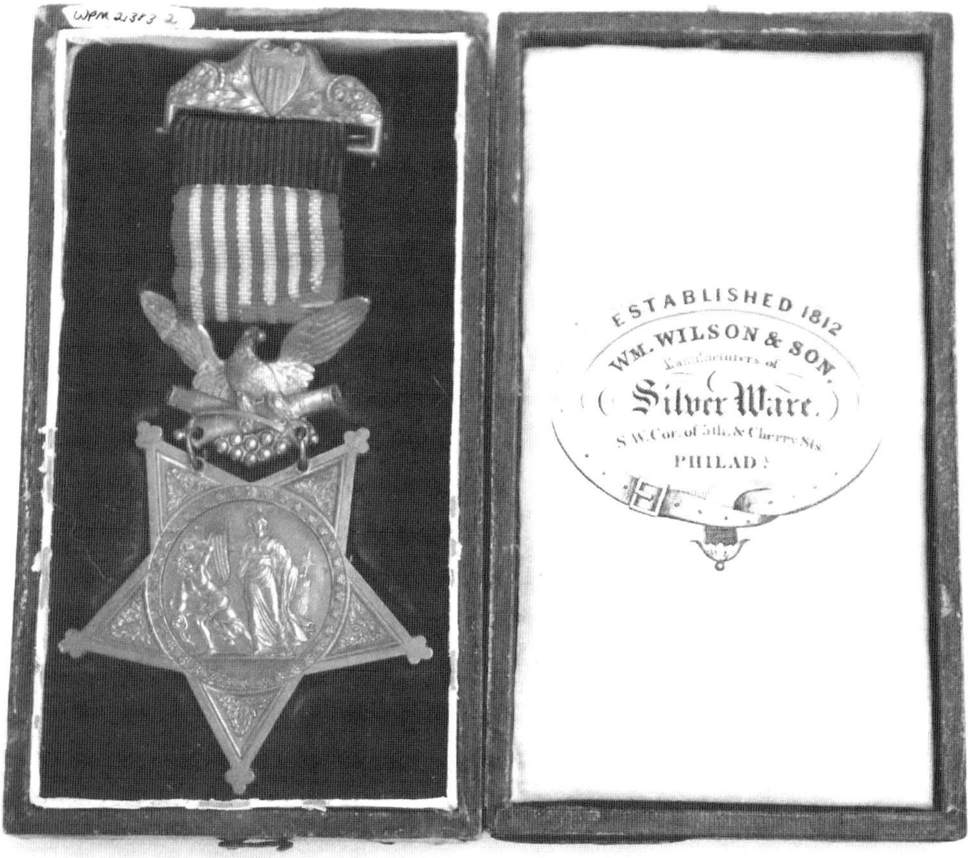

***Above*: Congressional Medal of Honour 1862-1896 issue.**
The highest award that can be bestowed for bravery in the United States, it was instigated during the American Civil War. *(Kind courtesy of West Point Museum Collection, U. S. Military Academy)*

***Left*: Indian Wars Campaign Medal.**
Awarded for the campaigns against hostile American Natives between 1865 and 1898, it was not authorised until January 1905. *(Author's Collection)*

he was annoyed at having to do so again. However, he also stated that he did not have a drink from the flask until midnight, when he was taking a break, and that his altercation with Churchill and Frett had taken place some hours previously. Other officers would confirm that he took a drink around midnight, although Captain French could not confirm that Reno had whiskey in his flask on the 28 June, when they were on the Custer battlefield, as French did not attend the inquiry to give evidence. Likewise, other witnesses could not confirm the packer's stories of Reno being drunk on the evening of the 25th June. Many had not heard anything of the incident until the spring of 1878 and that was from a scout, Fred Girard, who made no mention of it during his testimony. It seems that a veteran officer such as Reno would not have been intoxicated that evening, but the fact that he did carry a flask of whiskey and take an occasional drink from it was common practice on the frontier. Of course, it could also be argued that Churchill and Frett had collaborated with each other, or even with Whittaker to cloud the proceedings and put pressure on Reno. Whilst that might be an interesting thought, it cannot be proved and will remain unanswered.

Benteen's battalion had arrived on the bluff about twenty minutes after Reno's retreat from the valley and some considerable time before the arrival of the park train. Three of the battalion officers gave evidence, including Benteen himself. Of the two remaining officers who participated in the defence of the bluff, Captain Thomas Weir of Company D had died on 9th December of congestion of the brain and First Lieutenant Francis Gibson did not attend the inquiry. Gibson actually hated Reno, saying that he was arrogant and vicious, but at a later date he wrote that at the time of the inquiry he had thought about protesting against the accusation that Reno was a coward. In any event, he did nothing.

First Lieutenant Winfield S. Edgerly, had been a second lieutenant in Company D, under Captain Weir at the time of the battle. He began his testimony during the afternoon of Monday 3rd February. He narrated the events as far as his company was concerned and when asked about Reno's conduct over the two days of defensive action on the bluff, he replied that Major Reno was one of the first officers he encountered upon his arrival and that,

> "He was mounted: had lost his hat, and had a white handkerchief around his head. He was in an excited condition, and as we came up he turned and discharged his pistol towards the Indians 1,000 yards away."

Edgerly also added that though Reno had appeared excited it was not enough to impair his efficiency or have any adverse effect on the troops under his command. He said that he seen Reno walk through the lines as other officers had, and appeared very cool, exercising the functions of a commanding officer and he firmly verified that he had seen no evidence of cowardice on Reno's part during that period.

Edgerly's evidence is interesting, for he stated that not only had Reno lost his hat and was wearing a white handkerchief around his head, but that Second Lieutenant Charles Varnum had also lost his hat and was also wearing a white handkerchief around his head. Could the participants defending the bluff, engaged in a furious fight with the hostiles, amidst the smoke and dust, have mistaken one officer for the other at that time? It is a possibility, although it does not appear that any such mistake would have made any difference to the outcome of the inquiry. It does deserve some consideration though.

Captain Edward Godfrey had been a first lieutenant in command of Company K in June 1876 and was Recorder Lee's seventeenth witness to be called to the stand. Godfrey is another enigma of the era, a difficult personality to understand. Although he became a warm friend of Elizabeth Custer, his friendship did not stop him blaming her husband for the disaster and he did not believe that Major Reno was worthy of any praise either. At the inquiry Godfrey curtly stated:

> 'I was not particularly impressed by Reno's qualifications as to courage, coolness or efficiency…
>
> I don't think Reno's conduct was such as tended to inspire the command with confidence in resisting the enemy.'

It is interesting to note here that earlier in his career Godfrey had been accused twice of being inefficient and undisciplined, and both accusations had been brought against him by senior officers of the Seventh. Thus, Godfrey was hardly in a position to criticize Reno, yet he did several times in fact, in the articles and books that he wrote on the battle and the Indian Wars in general. Benteen was of the opinion that Godfrey's extensive authorship was just a way of capitalising on the misfortune of the Little Big Horn. Perhaps it was and his articles and books sold fairly well, but it did not deter from the fact that Godfrey's senior officers did not hold a very high opinion of him.

Captain Frederick Benteen, a battalion commander at the time of the battle, was Lee's fourteenth witness and he took the stand on Saturday

1st February. An intricate character, Benteen tantalizes the researcher with numerous ambiguous innuendoes that defy explanation. Some time after the court of inquiry, Benteen confessed that he could have said much more about the battle but the lawyers did not ask him the right questions. On 10th November 1891, he wrote to Theodore Goldin:

> 'Of course, I know a great many things about the fight that isn't essential that the world should know…'

Add these comments to those he made shortly after the battle and it leads to the assumption that Benteen had been forewarned of the conspiracy to deal with Custer. If that was the case, does that make him just as culpable as the conspirators or just an army officer who did not want to be 'dealt with' in the same manner as Custer had been? Were his senior officers wary of his connections in Washington or were they unsure of what he knew? In any event Benteen remained a captain until 1882, when he was finally promoted to major and he never did disclose his secrets which went with him to the grave. The fact that he did not rush to Custer's aid upon receiving the message only adds fuel to the speculations that surrounded Benteen and Whittaker may have been right in accusing him of failing to go to Custer's aid, but in all probability for the wrong reasons. Whittaker's reference to Benteen was dismissed by the presiding officers of the inquiry. They were there to investigate Reno not Benteen. Although not on the best of terms with Reno, when asked his opinion concerning the major's conduct, Benteen coolly replied,

> 'I think his conduct was alright…
> I saw no evidence of cowardice on Reno's part…'

He then compounded that statement with,

> 'I found it necessary at one point to caution him about exposing himself. I told him to be careful how he stood around, in front of the point, where we were making rifle pits, as volleys were coming constantly.'

The only other witness of Benteen's battalion who was called to testify was Trumpeter Giovanni Martini (John Martin) of Company H. Assigned to Custer's battalion as an orderly trumpeter, Martini only divulged his experiences and observations when delivering the last message to Benteen. He was not asked any questions regarding Reno's conduct by either Lee or Gilbert. Thus, his testimony is of little consequence to the inquiry but of enormous interest to later historians.

Reno's battalion, of course, had been the only command to have entered the battle from the start and, for the most part, to have emerged from it alive. His casualties had been severe, and included two officers: First Lieutenant Donald McIntosh and Second Lieutenant Benjamin Hodgson, both of whom had been killed. Captain Thomas French did not attend the inquiry as he was undergoing a court martial at Fort Leavenworth at that time. That left six officers, including Dr Porter, who had served under Reno's command during the battle and whose testimonies were, in some cases, vague and contradictory. It must have been very difficult for those witnesses to recall Reno's conduct in the valley and hilltop fights with any accuracy. Over two years had elapsed since the battle, during which time the Seventh had been engaged in other actions against hostile Indians and, it must be remembered, at the time of the battle at the Little Big Horn, these officers were not only trying to preserve their lives but those of their men as well.

First Lieutenant Charles De Rudio had become separated from the battalion during the retreat from the valley and did not re-join Reno on the bluff until the early hours of the morning of the 27th June. He was on foot with a private and they became lost amongst the gullies whilst evading the hostiles. Therefore, his testimony is not of much use to Reno and when asked his opinion concerning Reno's conduct, De Rudio replied that he had seen him on the skirmish line and had admired his conduct, adding,

> 'I saw no indication of cowardice on Reno's part; nor any want of skill in the handling and disposition of the men.'

Many did not regard De Rudio as a very efficient officer and he had been openly accused of 'hiding out' throughout the fighting to avoid any actual conflict with the hostiles.

Frederick Girard does not create much of an impression as a scout. Having also been separated from the troops during the retreat in the valley, he and another scout managed to catch some Indian ponies and they reached Reno's defence on the bluff some twenty-four hours after the fight, having got lost in the timber! Why he took so long to reach the bluff on a pony defies logic. He believed the soldiers could have held the timber position as long as they had plenty of ammunition and provisions, which they did not. Not being a soldier he would not have been aware of the logistical status of Reno's forces and he does not appear to have observed the movements of the hostiles very well either. Some scout!

Dr H.R. Porter not only had the wounded to care for but also had to preserve his own life as well. During the retreat from the valley he was observed galloping his horse as fast as any of the soldiers to escape the increasing Indians. Yet it appears he was able to escape and find the time to notice Reno's movements as well:

> 'I saw nothing in his conduct particularly heroic or particularly the reverse. I think he was somewhat a little embarrassed and flurried. The bullets were coming in pretty fast and I think he did not know whether it was best to stray there or leave.'

Porter may have run as fast as his horse could carry him to escape certain death, but his subsequent performance on the bluff in treating the wounded over the next two days was an enormous feat of medical devotion and human endurance that had largely gone unnoticed.

Second Lieutenant Charles Varnum was the third witness on Lee's list. Varnum had admired Custer and disliked Reno intensely, a fact that was clearly discernible in his non-committal testimony. He agreed that their position in the timber was precarious in view of the sudden escalation of the intensity of the fighting from the overwhelming numbers of the hostiles, adding:

> 'If Reno thought he could not hold the timber, and saw no troops coming, it was for him to use his own judgement and leave it for a place he could safely defend better.'

In other words, Reno was the commanding officer and it was his call. When asked to specify about Reno's conduct, Varnum replied:

> 'Certainly, there was no signs of cowardice or anything of that sort in his conduct and nothing special the other way.'

Luther Hare had only been commissioned as a second lieutenant in 1874 and was only 25 years old at the time of the battle. It was his first tour of duty in the field, not to mention his first contact with hostile Indians and as such, was very impressionable. Now a first lieutenant and a veteran of the Nez Perce War, Hare had obviously given some retrospective thought to the engagement and his testimony reflects that. Hare truthfully stated:

> 'I can only estimate his conduct by the way it turned out. I think his action saved what was left of the regiment.'

Hare also confirmed that he thought Reno's conduct was always good, that he seemed perfectly cool at all times and that he had seen no evidence of cowardice on Major Reno's part. However, he also commented that he had not seen anything particularly inspiring about the major's conduct either.

Captain Myles Moylan took the stand on the 24th January and continued to give evidence until 27th January. Although he was the brother in law of First Lieutenant James Calhoun, who had been killed with the Custer battalion, he was completely supportive of Reno's actions and decisions during the fight. Concerning the retreat from the timber, Moylan stated:

> 'If we had stayed thirty minutes longer in the timber, unsupported, I doubt whether we would have gotten out with as many as we did.'

Gilbert's cross-examination produced the same answer:

> 'In my judgement if Reno had continued to charge down the valley he would have been there yet…
>
> The purpose of leaving the timber was to save the command, which without assistance, would in my judgement, have been annihilated in the timber.'

On the question of Reno's conduct, Moylan was equally undeterred:

> 'Major Reno gave his orders during the advance in the bottom as coolly as any man under the circumstances. He was in front of the command all the time. During the afternoon of the twenty-fifth he seemed perfectly cool. I saw nothing to indicate cowardice.'

First Lieutenant George Wallace was the second witness that Lee called. His testimony began on the morning of Thursday 18 January and continued until the afternoon of Saturday 20th January, during which time he gave a highly detailed account of the valley and hilltop fights. Wallace had been a second lieutenant at the time of the fight and by the time it had ended, his company had sustained just under half its complement killed or wounded, including the commanding officer. In later years his testimony would become a prime source for researchers and there is little doubt that it helped to mould history's conception of the battle as a whole. It was during Wallace's testimony that reporting restrictions were lifted and the room rustled with movement as reporters hurriedly fumbled in their pockets for their notebooks and pencils. Wallace was positive in his evidence and unshaken during his cross-examination by Gilbert. When asked to recall his observations of Reno's conduct in the timber, Wallace was extraordinarily lucid in his reply stating:

> 'I think Reno did the only thing possible under the circumstances. If we had remained in the timber all would have been killed. It was his duty to take care of the command and to use his best judgement and discretion.'

With regard to Reno's overall conduct during the two days of fighting, Wallace was similarly adamant in his answer:

> Major Reno's conduct was all that could be expected from anyone…
>
> The troops could not have been handled any better…
>
> I think his conduct as to courage was good, I saw no evidence of fear then or at any time…
>
> I can recall no act of Major Reno during those two days that exhibited any lack of courage as an officer and a soldier, or that I can find fault with; nor lack of military skills.'

Only two enlisted men were called to give evidence (apart from Trumpeter Martini); Sergeant Ferdinand Culbertson of Company A, and sergeant Edward Davern. At the time of the battle Davern had been a Private of Company F assigned to Reno as an orderly, a detached duty that probably saved his life. Both their testimonies were very short and only pertained to Reno's conduct, of whom both men confirmed that they had seen no evidence of cowardice on the part of the major at any time.

Thus, amidst the quagmire of facts and distortions, the contradictory and sometimes vague testimonies, Reno appeared to have gained the upper hand in the affair. During the inquiry witnesses had varied the distances between key locations of the area and, despite vigorous efforts, Lee could not establish the exact times at which the described events had occurred. Even the newspaper reporters had noticed that those witnesses who had seen the same thing at the same time, gave completely different versions of the events. But that is human nature and police officers today will confirm that such conflicting evidence still helps to build the bigger picture. There had been only one thing that all the witnesses had agreed upon and that was the fact that Maguire's map was hopelessly inaccurate. However, it was another civilian witness who, once again, would attempt to strike a blow in Reno's direction.

George Herendeen had been a scout in Reno's battalion and had been the seventh witness to take the stand. Although he added very little to the evidence that had already been given, Herendeen stated that it was his opinion that the death of Bloody Knife and the wounding of a soldier whilst in the timber, had demoralised Reno and had precipitated a hasty retreat from the valley. Herendeen had actually opened a new line of questioning, but Lee did not pursue it and he did not ask him any specific questions concerning Reno's conduct. Had Lee tumbled the same animosity towards Reno that Herendeen appeared to share with Churchill, Frett, and Girard, all of whom were civilians? Whittaker's prime source of information had to have been obtained from somewhere and it had been these civilians that had circulated the unsubstantiated rumours that Reno had been drunk on duty. In any event, Lee did not push for any further information and Herendeen was dismissed.

Whittaker was furious at the punitive examination of Herendeen by Lee. He had extensively interviewed the scout in the past and felt sure that if the right questions were asked, Herendeen could condemn Reno. When the court resumed the following day, Whittaker requested that he be allowed to question Herendeen further. He had a list of questions prepared. Both Gilbert and Lee vigorously objected, which the court upheld, however Herendeen was recalled to the stand.

Lee asked Herendeen if it was his opinion that Reno had started the retreat under the influence of fear for his own safety, to which the scout replied:

> 'I judged the firing of that valley and the killing of that man was the cause of his starting.'

In his cross-examination, Gilbert was more skilful in asking specific questions and bluntly asked Herendeen:

> 'You formed your judgement of his cowardice by the volley that was fired that killed the Indian and wounded the white man before you left the timber?'

Herendeen appeared to have lost much of his confidence and replied:

> 'I am not saying that he is a coward at all.'

Whittaker was even more furious. His star witness had fallen. Of course, Whittaker had other sources for his libellous accusations and although it is believed some were enlisted men as well as civilians, his informants were never disclosed. He knew he had lost the contest.

Chapter 6

The Military Two-Step

Although the first courts of inquiry was recorded in 1757, very little is known about it and it has drawn little or no interest. Since then, there have been numerous courts of inquiry, deliberating on a diverse range of subjects including equipment failures and the conduct of serving officers, both the army and the navy. From the beginning such courts were not just judicial tribunals and could not act directly on their findings. They were convened to investigate the subject and determine whether or not further proceedings should be undertaken. Such courts were usually convened by the superior officers of the branch of service concerned, however, the court of inquiry of 1879 was unusual in that it had been formally requested by Major Marcus Reno, who sought an inquiry into his own conduct as an officer at the Little Big Horn in 1876.

Sherman had granted the request, but there is little doubt that he carefully orchestrated the whole proceedings from start to finish. It was in his interests to do so. The Reno Court of Inquiry was not a whitewash. It was a political statement that proved to the public at large that the Army did not cover up its mistakes or misdemeanours (not that the public were aware that they didn't in the first place, but it sounded good). It had been convened not to put Reno on trial, rather to exact the truth concerning the battle, which had already produced its heroes and villains.

During the weeks the inquiry had been in progress, Reno had sat with his lawyer listening to all the testimonies of the witnesses called, most of which had been irrelevant. Some time later Captain Benteen stated that there was so much more he could have divulged, but he was not asked the right questions! Does this suggest that the questions had been set prior to the court convening? A close examination of the transcript of the inquiry certainly suggests that is so. In any event, not one witness called actually accused Reno of cowardice or neglecting his duty. But still the major felt uneasy. As the final witness, Colonel John Gibbon, left the stand Reno asked the court if he could testify. He clearly felt that there were issues in the overall evidence that needed clarification. At first, he was refused, but Reno persisted and finally the officers presiding informed him that according to military procedure within the law, he would have to apply in writing if he wanted to expound on the testimonies already given (This was obviously filibustering to cloud the issue in the hope that Reno would not apply.) Reno did apply and addressing his request to 'the Honourable Court of Inquiry' he wrote:

> 'In accordance with the Act of Congress approved 16 March 1878 I have the honor (sic) to request that I be allowed to testify before your honourable (sic) Court of Inquiry upon my application.'

On Friday 7th February Reno took the stand and under the direction of his lawyer, he gave his version of the events starting with the re-organisation of the battalions by Custer and ending with the arrival of Terry. The retreat from the valley was the first prominent point he needed to clarify. He firmly stated that it was not cowardice that had prompted him to leave the timber. He could see no troops arriving to support him and the hostiles were rapidly increasing in numbers. Their position in the timber was just not tenable. He told the court that he had already decided to leave the timber before Bloody Knife was killed so, contrary to Herendeen's statement, it was not the death of that Indian scout that caused the retreat. He had already issued orders for the troops to form in columns of fours, stating:

> 'I thought it was my duty to give those men the best chance I could to save themselves…
>
> … and took the responsibility. When I left there, I acted on my best judgement and I think events proved I was right.'

Reno admitted that he had sustained numerous casualties during the retreat and went on to describe the events on reaching the bluff; Benteen's arrival; Weir's advance; this disposition of the wounded and their standing defence over the next twenty-four hours. He confirmed that he had a flask of whiskey that he kept in the inner breast pocket of his jacket. He also confirmed that he took a drink from his flask around midnight on 25th June, but he remained strictly sober all the time. His flask still contained whiskey on 28 June when he was on the Custer battlefield and Captain French had asked him for a drink. Reno stated that on 25th June he had found civilians skulking amidst the pack train. This had made him angry and he not only admitted striking one of them, he also said that he told the packer he would shoot him if he was found amongst the pack mules again. Cross-examined by Lee, Reno stated that his relations with Custer were friendly enough. Lee pushed a little harder and asked Reno whether he had confidence in his commanding officer or did he distrust him? Reno remained stolid and replied:

> '... I had known Gen. Custer a long time; and I had no confidence in his ability as a soldier.'

When Lee challenged Reno's decisions, the major replied:

> 'I consider that the results of the battle justified my every act, and with the same knowledge I then had, I would again do the same thing under the same circumstances.'

Under a redirection from his lawyer, Reno stated:

> 'I did everything I could to assist and co-operate with Gen. Custer as much as if he were my own brother...
>
> I feel that I did everything possible short of sacrificing my command.'

In summing up, Lyman Gilbert adroitly dismissed some of the evidence given, especially the two civilian packers who were the only witnesses to question Reno's sobriety. Others he praised for their incredible recollections of the events. Lee, on the other hand, appeared determined to question the testimonies of the officers. He stated that some of the testimonies were contradictory to the official reports that had been written shortly after the battle and he expressed his doubts concerning Reno's motives for abandoning his presence in the valley, which resulted in a dash for the bluffs. He also made a huge play on what he called the esprit de corps, which he felt had prevailed within the regiment over the period of time since the battle:

> 'There is necessarily in the minds of the participants a sort of community interest and most certainly their judgement

> and opinions cannot remain absolutely impartial. Especially is this liable to be the case after a long lapse of time when many things are forgotten—and opinions became insensibly modified and changed. Esprit de corps and the personal interest which witnesses feel—these may unconsciously shape their opinion or bias their judgement, and the testimony of impartial witnesses unbiased by either must always weigh heavily against such opinions.'

Lee was clearly not impressed and felt that Reno had not been completely exonerated of the charges against him, according to the testimonies they had dutifully recorded. He was particularly critical concerning the question of Custer being abandoned to his fate:

> 'The uncontradicted evidence shows that Gen. Custer did in point of fact receive no assistance from Major Reno, who was in command of fresh troops on the hill. The question as to culpable negligence is a matter of opinion.'

At a later date Lee was allegedly to have stated that the court had been imposed upon and that his own opinions had been completely altered. Perhaps he had by then realised his own inadequacies as a lawyer, in failing to extract more information from the witnesses, or perhaps he was just making excuses. Then there is the ever-powerful presence of General Sherman, who directed the proceedings as he saw fit, even to possibly altering the witness statements. In any event, the official transcript clearly indicates that Lee thought Reno was, indeed, guilty of the charges. But the final decision was not his to make.

On Monday 10th February, in accordance with the legal regulations, Lee and Gilbert filed their written speeches to the court, which was cleared whilst the presiding officers deliberated over the evidence and examined the arguments. It did not take long for King, Merritt, and Royall to reach their decision. To a silent audience the officers read their findings based, it was said, on the evidence given. After summarising the chronology of the battle and describing various aspects of it in relation to the testimony, the court concluded that:

> 'The defence position on the hill was a heroic one against fearful odds. The conduct of the officers throughout was

> excellent and while subordinates in some instances did more for the safety of the command by brilliant displays of courage than did Major Reno, there was nothing in his conduct which requires animadversion from this Court. It is the conclusion of this Court in view of all the facts in evidence, that no further proceedings are necessary in this case, and it expresses this opinion in compliance with the concluding clause of the order convening the Court.'

The transcript of the proceedings and the court's verdict were then forwarded to W.M. Dunn, the judge advocate general. On 21st February, Dunn added his recommendation that the conclusion of the court be approved. Addressed to George McCrary, the secretary of war, Dunn wrote:

> 'I have the honor (sic) to submit the record of the proceedings of a Court of Inquiry convened by order of the General of the Army at the request of Major Marcus A. Reno, 7th Cavalry, for the purpose of enquiring into that officer's conduct at the Battle of the Little Big Horn River on 25th and 26th days of June 1876.
>
> After daily sessions with scarcely an omission for twenty-six days, and the taking of much testimony, the Court arrived at conclusions which are set forth in length in the second volume of the record.
>
> The testimony taken by the Court has been examined with sufficient minuteness to justify, it is believed, an entire concurrence in the results reached…
>
> I concur with the Court in its exoneration of Major Reno of the charges of cowardice which has been brought against him, and in its conclusion that no further action is required.
>
> … the testimony makes it quite clear that no one belonging to that detachment imagined the possibility of the destruction of Gen. Custer's troops; nor had this idea suggested itself, does it seem to have been at any time within their power, fighting as they were for life under the attack of a body of Indians vastly outnumbering them, to go to his assistance.
>
> The common feeling was at the time one of anger with Gen. Custer for sending them into so dangerous a position and apparently abandoning them to their fate.

> The suspicion or accusation that Ge. Custer owed his death and the destruction of his command to the failure of Major Reno, through incompetency or cowardice, to go to his relief, is considered as set at rest by the testimony taken before the present Court.
>
> It is respectfully recommended that the conclusion of the Court be approved.'

Ironically, before the court of inquiry drew to a close, the participants in the drama were informed of another terrible military disaster where the soldiers were overwhelmed by incredibly large numbers of a supposedly inferior enemy. On 22nd January, approximately 1,800 British and Native troops were annihilated by an estimated 20,000 Zulu impi at Isandlwana in Zululand. Whereas Custer's defeat had been a carefully planned homicide, the British defeat was primarily due to complacency and incompetence of the commanding officer, Lord Chelmsford. However, both these defeats still continue to be compared and argued over to this day. For the officers attending the court of inquiry, news of Isandlwana must have shaken them to the reality of their own drama. Whether or not it made any difference to the conclusions of the court is a matter of conjecture.

Of course, Sherman would have to endorse the verdict and Dunn's recommendations before the documents were sent to the secretary of war. Sherman formally endorsed the papers on 5th March. Now he could forget the whole episode and lay the ghosts to rest. That same day McCrary approved the findings. Government documents can move fast when it is convenient for them to do so!

The military had been seen to execute their duty. The president was confident that justice had been done and the Democrats were silenced. Sherman must have been overjoyed that no further proceedings were deemed necessary as that would have entailed a court martial, where it would have been difficult to remain in control and other factors may have reared their heads. Reno was jubilant. He had effectively and publicly cleared his name. But, as always, not everyone was enamoured with the verdict. Elizabeth Custer was absolutely furious. She had supported the judicial action and had lost. However, her devotion to her husband knew no bounds and she devoted the rest of her life creating a legend. A legend that has lived on over the years and will continue to do so. She died in New York on 4th April 1938, only a few days before her ninety-third birthday, and was buried beside her beloved 'Autie' in the U.S. Military Academy Cemetery at West Point.

As for Whittaker, who had been so instrumental in his efforts to blame Reno for the loss of his hero, he condemned the army in the newspapers for its mishandling of the affair. However, it was all over and as the public interest waned, so did his efforts to exact justice as he saw it. Whittaker abandoned his crusade and returned to his literary interests. In 1889 he died of a self-inflicted gunshot wound, sustained when he fell down the stairs whilst carrying a loaded pistol. Like his *beau sabreur*, he died with his boots on and a gun in his hand.

The existence of a murderous conspiracy has always been present within the swirling myths and legends that surround the drama and the conclusions of the court of inquiry did little to belay those rumours. Over time the conspirators have covered their tracks and probably burnt any incriminating paperwork. But, however faint, the terrible trail is still there and can be carefully followed by the hungry historian. Letters and other papers can be found which help to piece the puzzle together, like the one sent to the eminent author Cyrus Townsend Brady by Edward S. Godfrey:

> '... Developments subsequent to the campaign or battle leave little doubt that General Terry had about him men or influences that were suspicious, inimical, or hostile to General Custer. I sincerely believe General Terry was too high minded knowingly to allow himself to be influenced by any sinister motive.'

PART TWO

'Here, in the waves and troughs of the plains,
Where the healing stillness lies,
And the cast, benignant sky remains
And the long days make wise–

Bless to our use the rail and the sun,
And the blind seed in its bed,
That we may repair the wrongs that were done
To the living and the dead!'

Rudyard Kipling

Chapter 1

The Organisation and Strength of 7th U.S. Cavalry on the 25th June 1876

The total compliment of the 7th U.S. Cavalry in June 1876 was forty-three officers and 793 enlisted men, however not all of these were present at the Little Big Horn. The official commanding officer, Colonel Samuel D. Sturgis, had still not taken up his duties and together with two senior majors, Merrill and Tilford, there were approximately 200 other officers and men who were absent for one reason or another. This was not uncommon on the frontier where personnel of all ranks could be seconded to headquarters or detailed to their duties and, of course, the regimental band had been left behind at the supply camp when the final march commenced.

In the absence of Sturgis, Lieutenant Colonel George A. Custer assumed command of the regiment as senior officer, a position he held until his death.

Complete records of the organisation and strength of the 7th Cavalry prior to the battle are somewhat vague and inconsistent. This list has been compiled from all available authentic sources, including official papers from the U.S. National Archives and private collections.

The casualty lists have been merged with the muster rolls and have been compiled from the official Army lists that were approved by the Adjutant General's office on 1st November 1978.

Legend:	DOW	Died of Wounds
	KIA	Killed in Action
	W	Wounded

The Custer Battalion

Headquarters & Staff				
Custer	George A.	Lt Colonel	Commanding	KIA
Cooke	William W.	1st Lt	Adjutant	KIA
Lord	George E.	Ass. Surgeon		KIA
Sharrow	William H.	Sgt. Major		KIA
Voss	Henry	Chief Trumpeter		KIA
Attached Civilians				
Bouyer	Mitch	Interpreter		KIA
Custer	Boston	Guide		KIA
Kellogg	Mark	News. Reporter		KIA
Reed	Henry A.	Unassigned		KIA
Company C				
Custer	Thomas W.	Captain	Commanding	KIA
Harrington	Henry M.	2nd Lt		KIA
Bobo	Edwin L.	1st Sgt		KIA
Finckle	George A.	Sgt		KIA
Finley	Jeremiah	Sgt		KIA
Foley	John	Cpl		KIA
French	Henry E.	Cpl		KIA
Ryan	Daniel	Cpl		KIA
Bucknell	Thomas J.	Trumpeter		KIA
Kramer	William	Trumpeter		KIA
King	John	Farrier		KIA
Howell	George	Saddler		KIA
Allan	Fred E.	Private		KIA
Brightfield	John	Private		KIA
Criddle	Christopher	Private		KIA
Eiseman	George	Private		KIA
Engle	Gustar	Private		KIA
Farrand	James	Private		KIA

Company C (*Cont.*)				
Griffin	Patrick	Private		KIA
Hathersall	James	Private		KIA
Lewis	John	Private		KIA
Meier	Frederick	Private		KIA
Meyer	August	Private		KIA
Phillips	Edgar	Private		KIA
Rauter	John	Private		KIA
Rix	Edward	Private		KIA
Russell	James H.	Private		KIA
St. John	Ludwick	Private		KIA
Shade	Samuel S.	Private		KIA
Shea	Jeremiah	Private		KIA
Short	Nathan	Private		KIA
Stuart	Alpheus	Private		KIA
Stungwitz	Ignatz	Private		KIA
Thadus	John	Private		KIA
Van Allen	Garret H.	Private		KIA
Warner	Oscar	Private		KIA
Wright	Willis B.	Private		KIA
Wyman	Henry	Private		KIA
Company E				
Smith	Algernon E.	1st Lt	Commanding	KIA
Sturgis	James G.	2nd Lt		KIA
Hohmeyer	Frederick	1st Sgt		KIA
James	William B.	Sgt		KIA
Ogden	John S.	Sgt		KIA
Brown	George C.	Cpl		KIA
Eagan	Thomas P.	Cpl		KIA
Mason	Henry S.	Cpl		KIA
Meyer	Albert H.	Cpl		KIA
McElroy	Thomas F.	Trumpeter		KIA
Moonie	George A.	Trumpeter		KIA
Baker	William H.	Private		KIA

Barth	Robert	Private		KIA
Boyle	Owen	Private		KIA
Brogan	James	Private		KIA
Conner	Edward	Private		KIA
Darris	John	Private		KIA
Davis	William	Private		KIA
Farrell	Richard	Private		KIA
Forbes	John S.	Private	AKA Hiley	KIA
Heim	John	Private		KIA
Henderson	John	Private		KIA
Henderson	Sykes	Private		KIA
Hieber	William	Private	AKA Huber	KIA
Knecht	Andrew	Private		KIA
Liddiard	Herod T.	Private		KIA
O'Conner	Patrick E.	Private		KIA
Rees	William H.	Private		KIA
Rood	Edward	Private		KIA
Schele	Henry	Private		KIA
Smallwood	William	Private		KIA
Smith	Albert A.	Private		KIA
Smith	James	Private	#1	KIA
Smith	James	Private	#2	KIA
Stafford	Benjamin	Private		KIA
Stella	Alexander	Private		KIA
Torrey	William A.	Private		KIA
Van Sant	Cornelius	Private		KIA
Walker	George P.	Private		KIA
Company F				
Yates	George W.	Captain	Commanding	KIA
Van W. Reily	William	2nd Lt.		KIA
Kenny	Michael	1st Sgt		KIA
Nursey	Frederick	Sgt		KIA
Vickory	John	Sgt		KIA
Wilkinson	John R.	Sgt		KIA

Company F (*Cont.*)				
Briody	John	Cpl		KIA
Coleman	Charles	Cpl		KIA
Teeman	William	Cpl		KIA
Way	Thomas N.	Trumpeter		KIA
Brandon	Benjamin	Farrier		KIA
Manning	James R.	Blacksmith		KIA
Atcheson	Thomas	Private		KIA
Brady	William	Private		KIA
Brown	Benjamin F.	Private		KIA
Brown	William A.	Private		KIA
Bruce	Patrick	Private		KIA
Burnham	Lucien	Private		KIA
Carney	James	Private		KIA
Cather	Armantheus	Private		KIA
Dohman	Anton	Private		KIA
Donnelly	Timothy	Private		KIA
Gardiner	William	Private	AKA John Gard.	KIA
Hammon	George W.	Private		KIA
Klein	Gustav	Private	AKA Nicholas K.	KIA
Kelly	John P.	Private		KIA
Knauth	Herman	Private		KIA
Lerock	William H.	Private		KIA
Liemann	Werner L.	Private		KIA
Lossee	William A.	Private		KIA
Madsen	Christian	Private		KIA
Milton	Francis E.	Private		KIA
Monroe	Joseph	Private		KIA
Omling	Sebastian	Private		KIA
Rudden	Patrick	Private		KIA
Saunders	Richard D.	Private		KIA
Siefous	Francis W.	Private	AKA Sicfous	KIA
Warren	George A.	Private		KIA

Company I				
Keogh	Myles W.	Captain	Commanding	KIA
Porter	James E.	1st Lt		KIA
Varden	Frank E.	1st Sgt		KIA
Bustard	James	Sgt		KIA
Morris	George C.	Cpl		KIA
Staples	Samuel F.	Cpl		KIA
Wild	John	Cpl		KIA
McGucker	John	Trumpeter		KIA
Patton	John W.	Trumpeter		KIA
Bailey	Henry A.	Blacksmith		KIA
Barry	John D.	Private		KIA
Broadhurst	Joseph F.	Private		KIA
Conners	Thomas	Private		KIA
Downing	Thomas P.	Private		KIA
Driscoll	Edward C.	Private		KIA
Gillette	David C.	Private		KIA
Gross	George H.	Private		KIA
Hetesimer	Adam	Private		KIA
Holcomb	Edward P.	Private		KIA
Horn	Marion E.	Private		KIA
Kelly	Patrick	Private		KIA
Lehman	Frederick	Private		KIA
Lehmann	Henry	Private		KIA
Lloyd	Edward W.	Private		KIA
McIllargey	Archibald	Private		KIA
Mitchell	John E.	Private		KIA
Noshang	Jacob	Private		KIA
O'Bryan	John	Private	AKA O'Brian	KIA
Post	George	Private		KIA
Parker	John	Private		KIA
Pitter	Felix J.	Private		KIA
Quinn	James	Private		KIA
Reed	William	Private		KIA

Company I (*Cont.*)				
Rossbury	John W.	Private		KIA
Symms	Darwin L.	Private		KIA
Thomas	Herbert P.	Private		KIA
Troy	James E.	Private		KIA
Von Bramer	Charles	Private		KIA
Whaley	William B.	Private		KIA
Company L				
Calhoun	James	1st Lt.	Commanding	KIA
Crittenden	John J.	2nd Lt		KIA
Butler	James	1st Sgt		KIA
Cashan	William	Sgt		KIA
Warren	Amos B.	Sgt		KIA
Gilbert	William H.	Cpl		KIA
Harrison	William H.	Cpl		KIA
Seiler	John	Cpl		KIA
Walsh	Frederick	Trumpeter		KIA
Heath	William H.	Farrier		KIA
Siemon	Charles	Blacksmith		KIA
Perkins	Charles	Saddler		KIA
Adams	George E.	Private		KIA
Andrews	William	Private		KIA
Assadaly	Anthony	Private		KIA
Babcock	Elmer	Private		KIA
Burke	John	Private	AKA O. Pardee	KIA
Cheever	Ami	Private		KIA
Crisfield	William B.	Private		KIA
Crowley	John L.	Private	AKA J. Duggan	KIA
Dye	William	Private		KIA
Galvan	James D.	Private		KIA
Graham	Charles	Private		KIA
Hamilton	Henry	Private		KIA
Harrington	Weston	Private		KIA
Haugge	Louis	Private		KIA

Hughes	Francis T.	Private		KIA
Kavanagh	Thomas G.	Private		KIA
Lobering	Louis	Private		KIA
McCarthy	Charles	Private		KIA
McGue	Peter	Private		KIA
Mahoney	Barth	Private		KIA
Maxwell	Thomas E.	Private		KIA
Miller	John	Private		KIA
O'Connell	David J.	Private		KIA
Reibold	Christian	Private		KIA
Roberts	Henry	Private		KIA
Rodgers	Walter B.	Private		KIA
Schmidt	Charles	Private		KIA
Scott	Charles	Private		KIA
Siemonson	Bent	Private		KIA
Snow	Andrew	Private		KIA
Tarbox	Byron L.	Private		KIA
Tessier	Edward D.	Private		KIA
Tweed	Thomas S.	Private		KIA
Vetter	Johann M.	Private		KIA

The Reno Battalion

Headquarter & Staff				
Reno	Marcus A.	Major	Commanding	
Hodgson	Benjamin	H. 2nd Lt	Adjutant	KIA
DeWolf	James M.	Act. Ass. Surgeon		KIA
Porter	Henry R.	Act. Ass. Surgeon		
Attached Soldiers				
Abbotts	Henry A.	Hosp. Atten.	Co.E	
Brenan	John	Private	Co.C	
Brown	Franz C.	Pvt clerk/Reno	Co.I	

Attached Soldiers (*Cont.*)				
Butler	James W.	Hosp. Atten.	Co.F	
Davern	Edward	Pvt. Orderly/ Reno	Co.F	W
Korn	Gustav	Private	Co.I	
Pandtle	Christopher	Hosp. Atten.	Co.E	
Attached Civilians				
Cross	William	Scout		
Dorman	Isaiah	Interpreter		KIA
Girard	Frederick F.	Interpreter		
Herendeen	George B.	Scout/Courier		
Jackson	William	Scout		
Reynolds	Charles A.	Scout/Guide		KIA
Company A				
Moylan	Myles	Captain	Commanding	
De Rudio	Charles C.	1st Lt		
Heyn	William	1st Sgt		W
Culbertson	Ferdinand A.	Sgt		
Easley	John T.	Sgt		
Fehler	Henry	Sgt		
McDermott	George M.	Sgt		
Dalious	James	Cpl		KIA
King	George H.	Cpl		DOW
Roy	Stanislaus	Cpl		
Hardy	William G.	Trumpeter		
McVeigh	David	Trumpeter		
Bringes	John	Farrier		
Hamilton	Andrew	Blacksmith		
Muering	John	Saddler		
Aller	Charles	Private		
Armstrong	John E.	Private		KIA
Bancroft	Neil	Private		
Baumgartner	Louis	Private		
Blair	Wilbur F.	Private		

Blake	Thomas	Private		
Bott	George A.	Private		
Conner	Andrew	Private		
Cowley	Cornelius	Private		
Diehle	Jacob	Private		W
Drinan	James	Private		KIA
Durselew	Otto	Private		
Foster	Samuel J.	Private		W
Franklin	John W.	Private		
Gilbert	John M.	Private		
Harris	David W.	Private		
Holmstead	Frederick	Private		W
Hook	Stanton	Private		
Jonson	Emil O.	Private		
Johnson	Samuel	Private		
McClurg	William	Private		
McDonald	James	Private		KIA
Moodie	William	Private		KIA
Nugent	William D.	Private		
Procter	George W.	Private		
Reeves	Francis M.	Private		W
Rollins	Richard	Private		KIA
Seayers	Thomas	Private		
Siebelder	Anton	Private		
Strode	Elijah T.	Private		W
Sullivan	John	Private		KIA
Tweetzer	Thomas P.	Private		KIA
Taylor	William O.	Private		
Weaver	Howard H.	Private		
Company G				
McIntosh	Donald	1st Lt	Commanding	KIA
Wallace	George D.	2nd Lt		
Botzer	Edward	1st Sgt		KIA
Brown	Alexander	Sgt		

Company G (*Cont.*)				
Considine	Martin	Sgt		KIA
Northeg	Orlans H.	Sgt		
Akers	James	Cpl		
Hagemann	Otto	Cpl		KIA
Hammon	John C.	Cpl		
Martin	James	Cpl		KIA
Dose	Henry C.	Trumpeter		KIA
Wells	Benjamin J.	Farrier		KIA
Taylor	Walter O.	Blacksmith		
Selby	Crawford	Saddler		KIA
Boyle	James P.	Private		W
Brinkerhoff	Henry M.	Private		
Campbell	Charles W.	Private		W
Dwyer	Edmond P.	Private		
Goldin	Theordore W.	Private		
Graham	Thomas E.	Private		
Grayson	Edward	Private		
Hackett	John	Private		W
Johnson	Benjamin	Private		
Lattman	John	Private		
Loyd	George	Private		
McCormick	Samuel D.	Private		
McDonnell	John	Private		
McEagan	John	Private		
McGonigle	Hugh	Private		
McGinnis	John J.	Private		KIA
McVay	John	Private		W
Moore	Andrew J.	Private		KIA
Morrison	John	Private		W
O'Neill	Thomas	Private	AKA Thos. Dean	
Petring	Henry	Private		W
Rapp	John	Private		KIA

Reed	John A.	Private		
Robb	Eldorado J.	Private		
Rogers	Benjamin	Private		KIA
Seaffemab	Henry	Private		KIA
Small	John R.	Private		
Stanley	Edward	Private		KIA
Stevenson	Thomas W.	Private		
Weiss	Markus	Private		
Wallace	John W.	Private		
Company M				
French	Thomas	Captain	Commanding	
Ryan	John M.	1st Sgt		
Carey	Patrick	Sgt		W
O'Hara	Miles	Sgt		KIA
McGlone	John	Sgt		
Weihe	Henry C.	Sgt		W
Cody	Henry M.	Cpl	AKA Scollin	KIA
Lalor	William	Cpl		
Stressinger	Frederick	Cpl	AKA Streing	
Fischer	Charles	Trumpeter		
Weaver	Henry C.	Trumpeter		
Donohue	John	Saddler		
Bates	Joseph	Private		
Braun	Frank	Private		DOW
Cain	Morris	Private		
Darcy	James W.	Private	AKA J. Wilbur	W
Davis	Henry H.	Private		
Gallene	John B.	Private	AKA Gallenne	
Golden	Bernard	Private		
Gordon	Henry	Private		KIA
Heid	George	Private		
Kavanagh	Charles	Private		
Klotzbucher	Charles	Private		KIA
Lorentz	George	Private		KIA

Company M (*Cont.*)				
Mahoney	Daniel	Private		
McHugh	Philip	Private		
Meier	John H.	Private		W
Meyer	William D.	Private		KIA
Moore	Hugh N.	Private		
Morris	William E.	Private		W
Newell	Daniel	Private		W
Neely	Frank	Private		
Pigford	Edward D.	Private		W
Robinson	William E.	Private		
Rutten	Roman	Private		W
Ryder	Robert	Private		
Rye	William W.	Private		
Seamans	John	Private		
Senn	Robert	Private		
Sevens	James W.	Private		
Siverton	John	Private		
Slaper	William C.	Private		
Smith	George E.	Private		KIA
Sniffen	Frank W.	Private		
Stratton	Frank	Private		
Summers	David	Private		KIA
Tanner	James J.	Private		KIA
Thornberry	Levi M.	Private		
Thorpe	Rollins L.	Private		
Turley	Henry J.	Private		KIA
Voight	Henry C.	Private		KIA
Varner	Thomas B.	Private		W
Weaver	George	Private		
Weeks	James	Private		
Weidman	Charles T.	Private		W
Whisten	John V.	Private		
Williams	Charles H.	Private		
Zametzer	John	Private		

The Benteen Battalion

Company D				
Weir	Thomas B.	Captain	Commanding	
Edgerly	Winfield S.	2nd Lt		
Martin	Michael	1st Sgt		
Flanagan	James	Sgt		
Harrison	Thomas W.	Sgt		
Russell	Thomas	Sgt		
Wylie	George W.	Cpl		
Bohner	Aloys	Trumpeter		
Charley	Vincent	Farrier		KIA
Deetline	Frederick	Blacksmith		
Myers	John	Saddler		
Alberts	James H.	Private		
Ascough	John B.	Private		
Brant	Abraham B.	Private		
Conlan	Thomas	Private		
Cox	Thomas	Private		
Dann	George	Private		
Dawsey	David E.	Private		
Fay	John J.	Private		
Fox	John	Private		
Golden	Patrick M.	Private		KIA
Green	Joseph H.	Private		
Hall	John C.	Private		
Hardden	William	Private		
Harris	James	Private		
Hayer	John	Private	AKA Hager	
Hetler	Jacob	Private		W
Holden	Henry	Private	AKA J. Hurd	
Horn	George	Private		
Houghtaling	Charles H.	Private		
Housen	Edward	Private	AKA Hansen	KIA
Hunt	George	Private		

Company D (*Cont.*)				
Kavanagh	James	Private		
Keller	John D.	Private		
Kipp	Freemont	Private		
Kretchmer	John	Private		W
McDonnell	Patrick	Private		W
Manning	David	Private		
Marshall	William A.	Private		
Meadwell	John	Private		
O'Mann	William	Private		
Randall	William J.	Private		
Reid	Elwyn S.	Private		
Sadler	William	Private		
Sanders	Charles	Private		
Scott	George D.	Private		
Smith	Henry G.	Private		
Smith	William E.	Private		
Stivers	Thomas W.	Private		
Tolan	Frank	Private		
Welch	Charles H.	Private		
Wynn	James	Private		
Company H				
Benteen	Frederick W.	Captain	Commanding Battalion	W
Gibson	Francis M.	1st Lt		
McCurry	Joseph	1st Sgt		W
Connelly	Patrick	Sgt		W
Geiger	George H.	Sgt		
McLaughlin	Thomas F.	Sgt		W
Moroney	Mathew	Sgt		
Pahl	John	Sgt		W
Bishop	Alexander B.	Cpl		W
Lell	George	Cpl		KIA
Nealon	Daniel	Cpl		
Martini	Giovanni	Trumpeter	AKA John Martin	

Ramell	William	Trumpeter		W
Mechlin	Henry W.	Blacksmith		
Voit	Otto	Saddler		W
Adams	Jacob	Private		
Bishley	Henry P.	Private		W
Bishop	Charles H.	Private		W
Black	Henry	Private		W
Channell	William	Private		
Cooper	John H.	Private		W
Day	John H.	Private		
Dewey	George W.	Private		
Diamond	Edward	Private		
Farley	William	Private		W
George	William M.	Private		DOW
Glease	George W.	Private		
Haley	Timothy	Private		
Hughes	Thomas	Private	AKA Chas. Hughes	W
Hunt	John	Private		
Kelly	George	Private		
Kelly	James	Private		
Jones	Julien D.	Private		KIA
Lawhorn	Thomas	Private		
McDermott	Thomas	Private		
McNamara	James	Private		
Meador	Thomas E.	Private		KIA
Moller	Jan	Private		W
Nees	Elder	Private		
Nicholas	Joshua S.	Private		
O'Ryan	William	Private		
Phillips	John J.	Private		W
Pinkston	John S.	Private		
Sevens	Samuel	Private		W
Williams	William C.	Private		W
Windolph	Charles A.	Private		W

Company K				
Godfrey	Edward S.	1st Lt	Commanding	
Winney	De Witt	1st Sgt		KIA
Campbell	Jeremiah	Sgt		
Fredericks	Andrew	Sgt		
Rott	Louis	Sgt		
Rafter	John	Sgt		
Callahan	John J.	Cpl		KIA
Hose	George	Cpl		
Penwell	George B.	Trumpeter		
Schlafer	Christian	Trumpeter		
Steinker	John R.	Farrier		
Burke	Edmund H.	Blacksmith		
Boissen	Christian	Saddler		
Blunt	George	Private		
Bresnaham	Cornelius	Private		
Brown	Joseph	Private		
Burkhardt	Cornelius	Private		
Chesterwood, Charles	Private			
Clear	Elihue F.	Private	AKA Clair	KIA
Voakley	Patrick	Private		
Corcoran	Patrick	Private		W
Delancy	Michael	Private		
Donohue	John F.	Private		
Foley	John	Private		
Gibbs	William	Private		
Gordon	Thomas A.	Private		
Helmer	Julius	Private		KIA
Jennys	Alonzo	Private		
Lasley	William W.	Private		
McConnell	Wilson	Private		
McCue	Martin	Private		

Madden	Michael P.	Private		W
Mielke	Max	Private		W
Murphy	Michael	Private		
Murphy	Thomas	Private		
Raichel	Henry W.	Private		
Robers	Jonathan	Private		
Shauer	John	Private		
Schwerer	John	Private		
Siefert	August	Private		
Wasmus	Ernest	Private		
Whitlow	William	Private		

The Pack Train Escort

Company B				
McDougall	Thomas M.	Captain	Commanding	
Hill	James	1st Sgt		
Criswell	Benjamin C.	Sgt		W
Hutchinson	Rufus D.	Sgt		
Murray	Thomas	Sgt		W
Cunningham	Charles	Cpl		W
Dougherty	James	Cpl		W
Smith	William M.	Cpl		W
Wetzel	Adam	Cpl		
Kelly	James	Trumpeter		
Moore	James E.	Farrier		
Crump	John	Blacksmith		
Bailey	John A.	Saddler		
Barry	Peter O.	Private		
Barsantee	James F.	Private		
Boam	William	Private		
Bonner	Hugh	Private		

Company B (*Cont.*)				
Boren	Ansgarius	Private		
Brainard	George	Private		
Callen	Thomas J.	Private		
Campbell	Charles A.	Private		
Carmody	Thomas	Private		
Casey	John J.	Private		
Clark	Frank	Private		
Coleman	Thomas W.	Private		
Criswell	Harry	Private		
Crowe	Michael	Private		
Crowely	Patrick	Private		
Davenport	William H.	Private		
De Voto	Augustus L.	Private		
Dorn	Richard B.	Private		KIA
Frank	William	Private		
Mack	George B.	Private		KIA
Martin	William	Private		
McCabe	John	Private		
McLaughlin	Terence	Private		
McMasters	William	Private		
O'Neill	John	Private		
Pym	James	Private		W
Randall	George F.	Private		
Ryan	Steven L.	Private		
Sager	Hiram W.	Private		
Shea	Daniel	Private		
Spinner	Phillip	Private		
Stout	Edward	Private		
Stowers	Thomas J.	Private		
Trumble	William	Private		
Wallace	Richard A.	Private		
Woods	Aaron	Private		

The Pack Train

Attached Military Personnel				
Mathey	Edward G.	1st Lt	Co.M	Commanding
Company C				
Kanipe	Daniel A.	Sgt		
Hanley	Richard P.	Sgt		
Fitzgerald	John	Farrier		
Bennett	James C.	Private		DOW
Fowler	Isaac	Private		
Jordan	John	Private		
Mahoney	John J.	Private		
McGuire	John B.	Private		W
Mullin	Martin	Private		
Nitsche	Ottacar	Private		
Watson	James	Private		
Thompson	Peter	Private		W
Whittaker	Alfred	Private		W
Company E				
Riley	James T.	Sgt		W
Spencer	Abel B.	Farrier		
Berwald	Frank	Blacksmith		
Miller	Henry	Blacksmith		
Shields	William M.	Saddler		W
Bromwell	Latrobe	Private		
Cunningham, Charles		Private		W
Farrar	Morris M.	Private		
James	John	Private		
Kim	John G.	Private		
Lang	Henry	Private		
McKenna	John	Private		
McNally	James P.	Private		
O'Toole	Francis	Private		
Reese	William	Private		

Company F				
Curtis	William A.	Sgt		
Schleiper	Claus	Saddler		
Finnegan	Thomas J.	Private		
Gregg	William J.	Private		
Howard	Frank	Private		
Hunter	Frank	Private		
Lefler	Meig	Private		
Lynch	Dennis	Private		
Lyons	Bernard	Private		
Moore	Lansing A.	Private		
Myers	Frank	Private		
Pickard	Edwin H.	Private		
Pilcher	Albert	Private		
Reiley	Michael	Private		
Rooney	James M.	Private		
Shutte	Frederick	Private		
Sweeney	John W.	Private		
Walsh	Thomas	Private		
Company I				
De Lacy	Milton	Sgt		
Braun	Franz C.	Private		
Cooney	David	Private		DOW
Kennedy	Francis J.	Private		
Johnson	Francis	Private		
Jones	Henry P.	Private		
McShane	John	Private		
Owens	N.G.	Private		
Ramsey	Charles	Private		
Company L				
Mullan	John	Sgt		
Abrams	William G.	Private		
Banks	Charles	Private		
Brown	Nathan J.	Private		

Burkman	John W.	Private		
Etzler	William	Private		
Logue	William J.	Private		
Marshall	Jasper	Private		W
McHugh	Phillip	Private		
Rose	Peter E.	Private		
Stoffel	Henry	Private		
Sullivan	Timothy	Private		
Attached Civilians				
Wagoner	John C.	Chief Packer		W
Alexander	William	Packer		
Churchill	Benjamin F.	Packer		
Edwards	George	Packer		
Flint	Moses E.	Packer		
Frett	John	Packer		
Lainplough	John	Packer		
Lawless	William	Packer		
Loeser	Chris	Packer		
Mann	Frank C.	Packer		KIA
McBratney	Harry	Packer		
Moore	Edward L.	Packer		

Indian Scouts

Varnum	Charles A.	2nd Lt	Co. A	Commanding	W
Hare	Luther R.	2nd Lt.	Co. K		
Arikara					
	Barking Wolf				
	Bey	Chief			
	Bear Come Out				
	Bear's Eyes				
	Bear Running in the Timber				
	Black Calf				

Arikara (*Cont.*)					
	Black Fox				
	Black Porcupine				
	Bloody Knife				KIA
	Bobtail Bull	Chief			KIA
	Bull				
	Bull in the Water				
	Bush	AKA Charging Bull			
	Climbs the Bluff				
	Curley Head				
	Foolish Bear				
	Forked Horn				
	Good Face				
	Goose				W
	Horns in Front				
	Howling Wolf				
	Laying Down				
	Left Hand				
	Little Brave				KIA
	Little Sioux				
	Long Bear				
	One Feather				
	One Horn				
	Owl	AKA Pretty Face			
	Red Bear				
	Red Foolish Bear				
	Red Star	AKA Red Wolf			

	Round Wooden Cloud				
	Running Wolf				
	Rushing Bull				
	Scabby Face				
	Soldier				
	Stab				
	Strikes the Lodge				
	Strikes Two				
	Wagon				
	White Cloud				
	White Eagle				
	Young Hawk				
Crow					
	Curley				
	Goes Ahead				
	Hairy Moccasin				
	Half Yellow Face				
	White Man Runs Him				
	White swan				

Chapter 2

The Native Indian Participants and Casualty Lists for 25th June 1876

As far as it is known, the hostile Indians did not suffer such terrible losses in their numbers compared with those of the military. Unfortunately, there are no official records of the hostiles who fought at the Little Big Horn and very few documents that detail those who were killed or wounded. However, there is much to tell the historian although it has to be painstakingly pieced together. The hostiles themselves made remarkable pictographs of the battle and these are a rich source of material. Then we have the notes of such researchers as Walter Camp, Thomas Marquis, Stanley Vestal and, of course, David Humphries Miller. All authentic prime sources have been scoured, including the military lists that were compiled when the hostiles eventually surrendered.

Of course, it must be borne in mind that the following names may not be entirely correct, for the Indians themselves changed their names numerous times and those writing the surrender lists may have misspelt names or did not hear the interpreters correctly. It is a veritable nightmare and these lists are by no means complete, just the tip of the iceberg, but they are a foundation from which to grow. I offer my sincere apologies to those I was unable to identify but they are remembered anonymously.

Legend:	DOW	Died of Wounds
	KIA	Killed in Action
	W	Wounded

Arapaho	Left Hand	
	Waterman	
	Well Knowing One	
	Yellow Eagle	

	Yellow Fly	
Blackfeet	Flying Charge	KIA
	Kill Eagle	
	Scabby Head	
Southern Cheyenne	Brave Bear	
	Bull Bear	
	Lame White Bull	
	Lame White Man	KIA
	Little Robe	
	Roman Nose	
	Sitting Bull	
	White Horse	
	White Shield	
	Wild Hog	
Northern Cheyenne	American Horse	
	Bad Horse	
	Bald Eagle	
	Bear Heart	
	Bear Trail	
	Bear Walks On Ridge	
	Bearded Man	KIA
	Beaver Claws	
	Big Beaver	
	Big Crow	
	Big Foot	
	Big Nose	
	Black Cloud	KIA
	Black Coyote	
	Black Grain	
	Black Horse	
	Black Kills	
	Black Knife	
	Black Moccasin	

	Black Shield	
	Black Stone	
	Black White man	KIA
	Black Wolf	
	Bobtail Horse	
	Box Elder	
	Braided Locks	W
	Brave Wolf	
	Broken Jaw	
	Brown Bird	
	Buffalo Calf	
	Buffalo Calf Road Woman	
	Bull Hump	
	Bullet Proof	
	Charcoal Bear	
	Closed Hand	KIA
	Comes In Sight	
	Contrary Belly	
	Corn	
	Crazy Head	
	Crazy Mule	
	Crooked Nose	
	Crow Necklace	
	Cut Belly	DOW
	Did Not Go Home	
	Dirty Moccasins	
	Dives Backwards	
	Dog Friend	
	Eagle tail Feather	
	Fast Walker	
	Flapping Horn	
	Flat Iron	
	Fleece	
	Flying By	

	Frog	
	Ghost Hide	
	Goes After Other buffalo	
	Grasshopper	
	Hanging Wolf	
	He Dog	
	High Bear	
	High Walking	
	Hollow Wood	
	Horse Road	
	Howling Wolf	
	Hump Nose	KIA
	Iron Shirt	
	Issues	
	Jealous Bear	
	John Two Moon	
	Joseph Eagle Chasing	
	Just walks	
	Kate Bighead	
	Kills In The Night	
	Kills many	
	Lame White Man	KIA
	Last Bull	
	Left Hand	KIA
	Left Hand Shooter	
	Lightning Killer	
	Limber Bones	KIA
	Limpy	
	Little Bear	
	Little Bird	W
	Little Coyote	
	Little Creek	
	Little Hawk	
	Little Horse	

	Little Shield	
	Little Sun	
	Little Wolf	
	Lone bear	
	Noisy Walking	KIA
	Old Bear	
	Old Man Coyote	
	Owns red Horse	KIA
	Pawnee	
	Pig	
	Pine	
	Plenty Bears	
	Plenty Crows	
	Plenty Of Buffalo Bull Meat	
	Porcupine	
	Powder Face	
	Raising Fire	
	Rattlesnake Nose	
	Red Cherries	
	Red Horse	
	Red Owl	
	Red Robe	
	Red Tomahawk	
	Rising Sun	
	Roan Bear	
	Roman Nose	KIA
	Ray Eagle Chasing	
	Samuel Shot At	
	Sand crane	
	Sand Stone	
	Scabby	
	Sits Beside His Medicine	
	Sleeping Rabbit	
	Snow Bird	

	Soldier Wolf	
	Spotted Blackbird	
	Spotted Elk	
	Spotted Hawk	
	Spotted Rabbit	
	Spotted Wolf	
	Squint Eyes	
	Star	
	Strong Left Hand	
	Sun Bear	W
	Swift Cloud	KIA
	Tall Bull	
	Tall Sioux	
	Tall White man	
	Tanglehorn Elk	
	Ties His hair	
	Touches His Grub	
	Tripe	
	Turkey Legs	
	Two Birds	
	Two Feathers	
	Two Moons	
	Walking Medicine	
	Walks last	
	Weasel Bear	
	Whirlwind	KIA
	White Bird	W
	White Body	
	White Buffalo Shaking Off The Dust	
	White Bull	
	White Cross Eye	
	White Elk	
	White Frog	
	White hawk	

	White Moon	
	White Wolf	
	Wolf Chief	
	Wolf Medicine	
	Wolf Name	
	Wolf Tooth	
	Wooden Leg	
	Wooden Thigh	
	Wounded Eye	
	Yellow hair	
	Yellow nose	
	Yellow Weasel	
	Young Little Wolf	
	Young Two Moons	
Dakota Sioux: Santee	Gray Earth track	
	Inkpaduta	
	Noisy Walking	
	Plenty Of Meat	
	Red Point	
	Walks Under The Ground	
Lakota Sioux: Brule	Buffalo Horse	
	Flying Chaser	
	Hollow Horn Bear	
	Red Hill	
	Two Eagles	
	Two Strikes	
Lakota Sioux: Hunkpapa	Afraid of eagles	
	Bad Soup	
	Bear Bonnet	
	Bear Ears	
	Bear Shield	
	Bear With Horns	KIA
	Black Moon	

	Blue Cloud	
	Blue Mountain	
	Broad Tail	
	Brown Back	
	Buffalo Calf Pipe	
	Crawler	
	Crow King	
	Elk Heart	W
	Elk Nation	
	Elk Stands Alone	KIA
	Flat Hip	
	Gall	
	Good Bear Boy	W
	Good Voice Elk	
	Grey Whirlwind	
	Grey Eagle	
	Hawk Man	KIA
	Hawk Stays Up	
	Her Eagle Robe	
	Horney Horse	
	Iron Cedar	
	Iron Elk	
	Iron Hawk	W
	John Sitting Bull	
	Jumping Bull	
	Knife King	W
	Little Bear	W
	Little Crow	
	Little Knife	
	Little Moon	
	Little Voice	
	Little Wolf	
	Lone Bull	
	Long Road	KIA

	Old Bear	
	Powder Side	
	Pretty Bear	W
	Rain In The Face	
	Rectum	KIA
	Red Face	KIA
	Red Horn Buffalo	W
	Shoots Walking	
	Sitting Bull	
	Spotted Horn Bull	
	Strong Dog	
	Swift Bear	KIA
	Two Bulls	
	White Buffalo Bull	KIA
	White Bull	KIA
	White Eyebrows	
	White Gut	
	White Hair On Face	
	Young Black Moon	KIA
	Young Hawk	
Lakota Sioux: Miniconjou	American Horse	
	Bear Lice	
	Beard	
	Big Ankles	
	Black Shield	
	Breech Cloth	KIA
	Buffalo Bull	
	Bull	
	Charging Hawk	
	Comes Flying	
	Crazy Heart	
	Crazy Horse	
	Crow Bow	

	Dewey Beard	
	Dog with Horns	KIA
	Dog Backbone	KIA
	Fast Bull	
	Fat On The beef	
	Feather Earing	
	Flying By	
	Foolish Heart	
	Good Fox	
	High Back	KIA
	Hump	W
	Hump Little Crow	
	Iron Star	
	Iron Thunder	
	Kills standing	
	Kingman	
	Lame Deer	
	Lame Red Shirt	
	Lights	
	Little crow	
	Lone Bull	
	Long Elk	KIA
	One Bull	
	One Horn	
	Red Horn Bull	
	Red Horse	
	Roman Nose	
	Spotted Elk	
	Standing Bear	
	Takes The Horses	
	Three Bears	DOW
	Touch The Clouds	
	Turtle Rib	
	White Bull	W

	White Hollow Horn	
	White swan	
	Wounded Hand	
Lakota Sioux; Oglala	American Horse	
	Around The Quiver	
	Ass Hole	
	At The End	
	Bad Hand	
	Bad Heart Bull	
	Bad Horse	
	Bad Light Hair	KIA
	Bad Miniconjous	
	Bad Partisan	
	Bad Sucker	
	Bear Horse	
	Bear Jaw	
	Bear Lying Down	
	Bear Star	
	Belly	
	Belly Full	
	Belly Inside	
	Big Belly Mule	
	Big Bend	
	Big Design	KIA
	Big eater	
	Big Elk	
	Big Lodge Chimney	
	Big Moon	
	Big Owl	
	Big Road	
	Black Bear	
	Black Bird	
	Black Elk	
	Black Eye lid	

	Black Fox	
	Black White Man	
	Bloody Knife	
	Blue Cloud	
	Blue House	
	Bluff	
	Brave Wolf	
	Bull Man	
	Bull Horn	
	Charging Hawk	
	Charging Shield	
	Chase In The Morning	
	Chief Man	
	Circling Hawk	
	Clown	
	Comes Again	
	Comes From War	
	Comes The day	
	Contrary	
	Crawler	
	Crazy Bear	
	Crazy Head	
	Crazy Heart	
	Crazy Horse	
	Cross Prick	
	Crossways	
	Crow dog	
	Dancing Arrow	
	Dog Ear	
	Dog Nothing	
	Don't Amount To Anything	
	Don't Get Out Of The Way	
	Dried Lake	
	Dried Prick	

	Duck Belly	
	Eagle Bear	
	Eagle Elk	
	Ear-Ring Prick	
	Enemy	
	Face Turner	
	Fast Horn	
	Fast Thunder	
	Fat Rump	
	Fears Nothing	
	Feather Moon	
	Fills the pipe	
	Fills Up	
	Flying By	
	Flying Hand	
	Flying Hawk	
	Foolish Elk	
	Four Bullets	
	Four Crows	
	Gets Together	
	Gives Out	
	Good Boy	
	Gopher	
	Grandfather	
	Greases His Arm	
	Hairy	
	Hangs His Head	
	Hard To Hit	
	He Dog	
	Heap Bear Lays down	
	High Eagle	
	Hoarse	
	Hole In The Face	
	Hollow Sunflower	

	Horn Chips	
	Horned Horse	
	Horse Bear	
	Hurts The Enemy	
	Iron Horse	
	Iron Magpie	
	Iron White man	
	Iroquois Limitation	
	Jack Red Cloud	
	John Con Roy	
	Kicking Bear	
	Kills At Night	
	Kills Enemy In Winter	
	Kills The Married	
	Knife	
	Knife Chief	W
	Lays Laughing	
	Likes To Fight	
	Little Back	
	Little Big Man	
	Little Boy	
	Little Buck	
	Little Bull	
	Little Hawk	
	Little Prick	
	Little Warrior	
	Living Bear	
	Loafer	
	Lone bear	
	Many Lice	KIA
	Nose In Sight	
	Old	
	One Brings Shit Far away	
	One Grass	

	One Kills At Eight Steps	
	One Teat	
	One That Steals	
	One Who Walks With The Stars	
	Owl Bull	
	Owns Arrow	
	Painted Brown	
	Pemmican	
	Pisses In The Horn	
	Plenty Dogs	
	Plenty Lice	KIA
	Plenty Shells	
	Poor Bear	
	Poor Dog	
	Pretty Legs	
	Pulls Out	
	Pumpkin Hill	
	Red Cloud	
	Red Crane	
	Red Dog	
	Red Feather	
	Red Hawk	
	Red Horn Buffalo	W
	Red Owl	
	Red Rock	
	Red Shirt	
	Red Tail	
	Ree	
	Rider	
	Robe Hair Outside	
	Runner	
	Running Eagle	
	Runs Close To Camp	
	Runs Fearless	

	Runs On Top	
	Saddle	
	Scabby Face	
	Scabby Place	
	Scaring Bear	
	Sees The Crow	
	Shave Elk	
	Shits On His Head	
	Shits On The Eagle	
	Shoots Walking	
	Short	
	Short Brule	
	Short Bull	
	Side Rib	
	Silas Blind	
	Singing Bear	
	Singing Prick	
	Sits Up Above	
	Sitting Bear	
	Sitting Elk	
	Sitting Hawk	
	Sitting Horse	
	Skunk Guts	
	Skunk Head	
	Sleeps There	
	Slow White Cow	
	Snake creek	
	Snatch Looser	
	Snatch Stealer	
	Soft Prick	
	Soldier	
	Soldier Hawk	
	Spotted Hand	
	Spread Pine	

	Spunker	
	Stands First	
	Stinking Tie	
	Strong Elk	
	Strong Fox	
	Tall Bull	
	Tanned Nuts	
	The Bud	
	The Bugger	
	The Bull	
	The Chief	
	The Hand	
	The Hill	
	The last	
	The Lights	
	The Rump	
	The Shield	
	The Whore	
	Three Hawks	
	Thunder Hawk	
	Thunder Tail	
	Tobacco	
	Top Lodge	
	Torn Belly	
	Tripe Fold	
	Two Face	
	Undone	
	Walking White cow	
	Walks In Mud	
	War Club	
	War Shanty	
	Warms His Blanket	
	Water Snake	
	Whistler	

	White Bear	
	White Cloud	
	White Cow Bull	
	White Dress	KIA
	White Face	
	White Hair	
	White Rabbit	
	White star	
	White Twin	
	Woman Bone	
	Wood Boat	
	Wood Root	
	Wounded In Back	
	Wrinkled Face	
	Wrinkler	
	Yellow Horse	
	Yellow Left	
	Yellow Robe	
	Young Man Afraid Of His Horse	
	Young Sitting Bull	
	Young Skunk	KIA
Lakota Sioux: Sans Arc	Black Eagle	
	Blue Coat	
	Cloud Man	KIA
	Crow Boy	
	Deeds	
	Eagle Hat	KIA
	Elk Bear	KIA
	Elk Head	
	Fast Bear	
	High Bear	
	High Elk	KIA
	High Horse	
	Hollow Horns	

	Iron Whiteman	
	Kills Him	KIA
	Lone Dog	KIA
	Long Robe	KIA
	One Dog	
	Pants	
	Red Bear	
	Spotted Eagle	
	Standing Elk	KIA
	Two Bears	KIA
	Yellow Cloud	
Lakota Sioux: Two Kettle	Chased By Owls	KIA
	Runs The Enemy	
Nakota Sioux	Two Bulls	
	White Eagle	
Unspecified Lakota	Bad Warrior	
	Bear Chasing	
	Bear King	
	Bear Soldier	
	Bear's Cap	
	Big Leggins	
	Big Nose	
	Black Body	
	Black Fox	KIA
	Black Prairie Dog	
	Black Tongue	
	Black Twin	
	Blind Water	
	Bobtail Bull	
	Brave	
	Brave Crow	
	Brave Hawk	
	Brings Plenty	
	Brown Wolf	

	Bull Eagle	
	Burst Thunder	
	Circling Hawk	
	Crazy Hawk	
	Cross Bear	
	Dog	
	Eagle Chase	
	Eagle Man	
	Eagle Thunder	
	Eugene Little Soldier	
	Fat Bear	
	Fine Weather	
	First Eagle	
	Foolish Bull	
	Four Horses	
	Stomach	
	Good Dog	
	Good Weasel	
	Hairy Chin	
	Has Horn	
	Henry Bear Thunder	
	High Eagle	KIA
	Horseshoe	
	Iron Bull	
	Iron Lightning	
	Iron People	
	John Crow	
	Joseph Warrior	
	Kills Alive	
	Kills Hawk	
	Little Dog	
	Little Eagle	
	Little Horse	
	Old Bull	

	One Elk	
	Own Bobtail Horse	
	Owns Horn	
	Paul Fat Clown	
	Pretends Eagle	
	Puts On His Shoes	
	Raised Him	
	Rattling Hawk	
	Red Bird	
	Red Fish	
	Round Fool	
	Scar Leg	
	Scarlet Bear	
	Scarlet Eagle	
	Scarlet Thunder	
	Shell Necklace	
	Shoots Bear As He Runs	
	Shot In The Face	
	Spotted Rabbit	
	Standing Black Bear	
	Standing Elk	
	Stands Straddle	
	Swift Bear	
	Tall Bull	
	The Man Who Walks With His Dogs	
	Thin Elk	
	Useful Heart	
	Whirling	
	White Beard	
	White Bird	
	White Buffalo	
	White Cow Walking	
	White Face Bear	

	White Hawk	
	White Horse	
	With Horns	
	Worm	
	Wounded Lice	
	Yellow bear	
	Yells At Daybreak	
	Young Bear	KIA
	Young Eagle	

Chapter 3

The Congressional Medal of Honour

The Congressional Medal of Honour is the highest award the United States of America can confer upon military personnel and was originally established on 12th July 1862, to be awarded to enlisted men and non-commissioned officers,

> '...who shall most distinguish themselves by their gallantry in action, and other soldier like qualities.'

Designed by Christian Schussel and engraved by Anthony C. Paquet, of the U.S. Mint in Philadelphia, 2,000 medals were struck by William Wilson & Sons once an appropriation fund of $10,000 had been established by Congress.

On 3rd March 1863, just twenty-two days before the first medal was awarded to Private Jacob Parrott of the U.S. Army Volunteers, the original statute was amended to allow officers to be eligible for the award and the appropriation fund was increased accordingly:

> '...That the President causes to be struck from the dies recently prepared at the United States Mint for that purpose, 'Medal of Honor (sic)' additional to those authorised by the act (resolution) July twelfth, 1862 and present the same to such officers, non-commissioned officers and privates as have most distinguished or who may hereafter most distinguish themselves in action: and the sum of twenty thousand dollars is hereby appropriated out of the monies from the treasury not otherwise appropriated to defray the expenses of the same.'

Thus it was on 10th May 1863, Second Lieutenant Thomas Ward Custer of Company B, 6th Michigan Cavalry was awarded the first of his two Medals of Honour. Like so many others who received the medal during the Civil War, his citation simply read:

> 'Capture of flag.'

His second award appears to be more deserving. His citation for 6th April 1865, whilst engaged at Sailors Creek in Virginia, states:

> 'Leaped his horse over the enemy's works and captured two stands of colours, having his horse shot under him and receiving a severe wound.'

Thomas Custer persisted in constantly wearing his two Medals of Honour with pride on his tunic, much to the annoyance of his brother George, who had not been awarded one.

Cast in bronze, the medal was an inverted star with a mixture of laurel leaves (representing victory) and oak leaves (representing strength) on each of the five points. The obverse displays a central design within a circle of thirty-four stars, each one representing a state. The central motif depicts Minerva, the Roman goddess of wisdom and war, defeating an enemy representing Discord, which was a fitting if not symbolic statement considering the times in which the medal had been designed. Minerva is wearing a helmet upon which is perched an owl signifying wisdom and in her left hand she holds the 'fasces', the Roman symbol of authority that consisted of an axe bound with staves of wood. In her right hand Minerva holds a shield against Discord, who cowers beneath it clutching snakes in his hand. The reverse was inscribed 'Personal Valor' (sic) with the remaining space left blank for the name of the recipient and the date and place of the deed.

The bronze star was suspended from a ribbon by an eagle on the top of two crossed cannon, mounted on eight cannon balls and holding a sabre in its claw. The ribbon had a deep blue bar across the top, beneath which were thirteen vertical stripes; seven red and six white to symbolise the number of the original colonies that first formed the United States of America. The clasp was mounted behind the shield of the United States, this being flanked by filigree, from which the medal ribbon was suspended.

By its very nature the Battle of the Little Big Horn was bound to make the news, however, in view of the participants who were killed, it made the headlines across the nation and caused a sensation. It was not surprising then, that on 26th February 1878 the War Department received recommendations from company commanders for awards to be issued to named personnel for their conspicuous gallantry during the fight. These were endorsed by their area commander, Brigadier General Alfred Terry. These selections must have been extremely difficult to produce, for subsequent research has shown that all the soldiers had endured an exceptionally traumatic fight and they had all played equal parts in the terrifying drama. The list provided was carefully examined and on 8th September 1878 Adjutant General R.C. Drum, of the War Department, made his request for Medals of Honour to be awarded to the named enlisted men of the Seventh Cavalry. No less than twenty-four of these prestigious medals were issued, although none were awarded to any of the officers involved. Their names, together with their citations are as follows:

The Reno Battalion

Company A

Corporal Stanislaus Roy
Date of award: 5th October 1878
'Brought water to the wounded at great danger to life and under a most galling fire of the enemy.'
Private Neil Bancroft
Date of award: 5th October 1878
'Brought water for the wounded under a most galling fire.'
Private David Harris
Date of award: 5th October 1878
'Brought water for the wounded, at great danger to his life, under a most galling fire from the enemy.'

Company G

Private Theodore W. Goldin
Date of award: 21st December 1895
'One of a party of volunteers who, under a heavy fire from the Indians, went for and brought water for the wounded.'

The Benteen Battalion

Company D

Blacksmith Frederick Deetline
Date of award: 15th October 1878
'Voluntarily brought water to the wounded under fire.'

Private Abram B. Brant
Date of award: 5th October 1878

'Brought water for the wounded under a most galling fire.'
Private William M. Harris
Date of award: 5th October 1878
'Voluntarily brought water for the wounded under fire of the enemy.'

Private Henry Holden
Date of award: 5th October 1878
'Brought up ammunition under a galling fire from the enemy.'

Private George D. Scott
date of award: 5th October 1878
'Voluntarily brought water to the wounded under fire.'

Private Thomas W. Stivers
Date of award: 5th October 1878
'Voluntarily brought water to the wounded under fire.'

Private Frank Tolan
date of award: 5th October 1878
'Voluntarily brought water to the wounded under fire.'

Private Charles H. Welch
Date of award: 5th October 1878
'Voluntarily brought water to the wounded under fire.'

Company H Sergeant George Geiger
Date of award: 5th October 1878
'With three comrades during the entire engagement courageously held a position that secured water for the command.'

Blacksmith Henry W.B. Mechlin
Date of award: unknown
'With three comrades during the entire engagement courageously held a position that secured water for the command,'

Saddler Otto Voit
Date of award: 5th October 1878
'Volunteered with George Geiger, Henry Mechlin and Charles Windolph to hold an exposed position standing erect on the brow of the hill facing the Little Big Horn River. They fired constantly in this manner for more than 20 minutes diverting fire and attention from another group filling canteens of water that were desperately needed.'

Private Charles A. Windolph
date of award: 5th October 1878
'With three comrades, during the entire engagement, courageously held a position that secured water for the command.'

The Pack Train

Company B Sergeant Benjamin C. Criswell
Date of award: 5th October 1878
'Rescued the body of Lieutenant Hodgson from within the enemy's lines; brought up ammunition and encouraged the men in the most exposed positions under heavy fire.'

Sergeant Rufus D. Hutchinson
Date of award: 5th October 1878
'Guarded and carried wounded, brought water for the same, and posted and directed the men in his charge under galling fire from the enemy.'

Sergeant Thomas Murray
Date of award: 5th October 1878
'Brought up the pack train, and on the second day the rations, under a heavy fire from the enemy.'

Corporal Charles Cunningham
Date of award: 5th October 1878
'Declined to leave the line when wounded in the neck during heavy fire and fought bravely all next day.'

Private Thomas J. Callen
Date of award: 24th October 1896
'Volunteered and succeeded in obtaining water for the wounded of the command; also displayed conspicuously good conduct in assisting to drive away the Indians.'

Private James Pym
Date of award: 5th October 1878
'Voluntarily went for water and secured the same under heavy fire.'

Company C Sergeant Richard P. Hanley
date of award: 5th October 1878
'Recaptured, single handed and without orders, within the enemy's lines and under a galling fire lasting some 20 minutes, a stampeded pack mule loaded with ammunition.'

Private Peter Thompson
Date of award: 5th October 1878
'After having voluntarily brought water to the wounded, in which effort he was shot through the head, he made two successful trips for the same purpose notwithstanding remonstrances of his Sergeant.'

Additional Notes

1. The ranks of the recipients have been listed according to the date of the action, as recorded in the official muster rolls, and not according to the date the medal was awarded. Thus, although Charles H. Welch of Company D had attained the rank of sergeant by the date of the award, he was still a private at the time of the battle and has been listed as such.
2. Private Thomas W. Stivers has been listed on the Medal of Honour Roll as Thomas W. Stevens. However, according to the regimental muster roll, he is listed as Thomas W. Stivers. Subsequent research has established that the two surnames do refer to the same man.
3. Saddler Otto Voit was wounded during the battle, as some of the others were who also received the Medal of Honour.

Chapter 4

The Indian Campaign Medal

The Indian Campaign Medal was awarded to all military personnel who participated in the numerous engagements with hostile Indians from 1865 to 1898, a span of thirty-three years.

The medal was authorised by a War Department General Order, Number 12, in 1907, and due to the lateness of its establishment, a huge number were issued posthumously. Cast in bronze, the initial ribbon was plain red, (the correct term being 'Old Glory Red,) however, even though the medal could not be confused with the French 'Legion of Honour', the ribbon itself was almost identical, even to the shape. Thus, in December 1817, two vertical black stripes were added.

The bronze medal is 3.2 cm in diameter and 0.2 cm in thickness. The centre of the obverse displays a mounted Indian wearing a war bonnet and carrying a lance. Centralised above the Indian are the words 'INDIAN WARS'. Centralised below the Indian is a buffalo head with a conventional arrangement of arrow heads completing the outer circle on each side with the wording at the top. The centre of the reverse depicts a spread eagle surmounted on a trophy consisting of a cannon, with six rifles and four standards. The eagle is holding an Indian shield and directly beneath the centre piece are the words: 'FOR SERVICE.' The top half of the outer circle above the eagle are the words: 'UNITED STATES ARMY.' The lower half of the outer circle, below the eagle, is completed by interlocked stars.

The ribbon is 3.5 cm in width and 3.4 cm deep. It is composed of the following arrangement of vertical stripes:

0.6 cm	Old Glory Red
0.5 cm	Black
1.4 cm	Old Glory Red
0.5 cm	Black
0.6 cm	Old Glory Red

Campaign streamers are constructed in the same design as the medal ribbon and display the particular campaign the regiment participated in through the centre. (For the 'Little Big Horn' the letters are yellow.) Originally, American Military services displayed their battle honours on the regimental colours and as many incorporated on the Nation Flag. It was considered by some that such decoration was defacing the national symbol, so on 7th February 1890, engraved silver bands were authorised to be attached to the wooden staff. However, due to a shortage of these silver bands in 1918, General John Pershing was authorised by the War Department to procure ribbon as a substitute, using the same colours as shown on the campaign medal, and to inscribe the battle honours through the centre awarded to the regiment concerned. Hand embroidered streamers were introduced on 3rd June 1920 and have continued to the present day. The current dimensions of a campaign streamer that is attached to the regimental colour just below the finial are: 6.8 cm in width and 91 cm in length, with a swallow tail end.

Acknowledgements

Considering this book has taken over thirty years to research, prepare, and write, it is obvious that I had a great deal of help from numerous people in the United States who were so eager to help. I cannot name you all, but you have my sincere thanks for the invaluable work you have done on my behalf. Thank you all.

When I first started this project there was no internet and information had to be gathered by post or over the telephone and as the information I was seeking could only be found in the United States, it became a very costly and lengthy process. I give my sincere thanks to all those whose patience with me and their own perseverance that has helped make the project into this book.

The National Archives in Washington DC were extremely helpful and my thanks are due to Elaine Everly of the Navy and Army Branch, as well as Paul Guite. The department of the army willingly stepped in to help, although I am sure they viewed me as an 'English nutcase'! I therefore thank Colonel Robert Waggoner, Richard Sommers, and Renee Klish for their painstaking help over some period of time. Of course, no book on this subject would be complete without the input of Neil Mangum, Park Ranger and Historian of the battlefield. I thank you so much. The 'Godfrey/Asbury' letter was chased across the States of the Midwest until it was found and I was sent a copy. I thank everyone involved in that chase, especially Allan Clark of the Eastern Montana College. Absolutely amazing!

Photographs and paintings are of prime importance in a book on this subject. My sincere thanks go to the grand-nephew of George A. Custer, Colonel Charles Custer, who has graciously given his permission to use his painting of the battle from his collection. Sam Cahoon was a brilliant inspiration and I thank him for his permission to use his beautiful photographs of the Little Big Horn to help illustrate the text. My thanks are also due to Todd Strand for his permission to use his photographs which were obtained through James Davis of the State Historical Society of North Dakota. Thank you all so much.

Research on the firearms in use during this period was helped by William Meuse of the Springfield Armoury National Site and L.K. Goodstal of the Remington Arms Co. Gun Museum, not to mention G.M. Wilson of the Armouries Museum, H.M. Tower of London (before it was moved to Leeds), who opened his office for me to see the army Colt that they had and which I duly photographed. Thank you for giving your time to instruct me and discuss the weapon.

My sincere thanks must go to Lawrence Frost, a genuine historian of Custer and the battle, who kept my enthusiasm for the project going with his correspondence, which I will always cherish.

Above all I submit my sincere thanks to Tara and Harriet at Pen & Sword Books Ltd for believing in my research and their invaluable help in putting my work into production.

Finally, I thank my family with all my heart for putting up with my research for so long and who believed in me so fervently, although I don't think they ever thought the project would ever be completed!

My love and sincere thanks to you all.

Selected Bibliography

ABRAMS, MARC H., *Sioux War Dispatches,* Westholme Publishing: USA: 2012

AGONITO, ROSEMARY, *Buffalo Calf Road Woman,* TwoDot: Montana: 2006

ALLISON, E.H., *Surrender of Sitting Bull,* South Dakota Historical Collection Vol.6: 1912

AMBROSE, STEPHEN, *Crazy Horse and Custer*, Simon & Schuster U.U. Ltd: London: 2003

ANDREWS, RALPH, *Curtis' Western Indians*, Bonanza Books: New York: 1962

ANDRIST, RALPH K., *The Long death*, Macmillan Publishing Co.: New York: 1964

ANGLO, MICHAEL, *Custer and the Myth*, Jupiter Books: 1977

ARMSTRONG, VIRGINIA I., *I Have Spoken*, Sage Books: Chicago: 1971

BAILLY, EDWARD, *Echoes from Custer's Last Fight*, 'Military Affairs': Winter: 1958

BARRETT, S.M., *Geronimo*, Sphere Books: London: 1970

BENTEEN, FREDERICK, *An Account of the Little Big Horn Campaign*, Ghent Paper: Washington: 1876

Letters to Edward W. Field 8 – 2 – 1886, Military Research Collection: Carlisle Barracks

Letters to Theodore W. Goldin 1891 – 1896, Military Research Collection: Carlisle Barracks

The Custer Fight, Hollywood: 1933

BLISH, H.H., *A Pictographic History of the Oglala Sioux*, Lincoln: Nebraska: 1967

BRADY, CYRUS T., *Indian Fights and Fighter*, University of Nebraska Press: Nebraska: 1971

BRANDON, WILLIAM, *The Rise and Fall of the North American Indians*, Tempus Publishing: Stroud: 2007

BRININSTOOL, E.A., *A Trooper with Custer*, Cooper Square: New York: 1975

Fighting Indian Warriors, Indian Head Books: New York: 1995

Troopers with Custer, Stackpole Books: Mechanicsburg: 1994

BRITT, ALBERT, *Great Indian Chiefs*, New York: 1938

BRITTON, JACK, *United States Military Medals & Decorations*, MCN Press: Oklahoma: 1979

BROOME, JEFF, *Dog Soldier Justice*, University of Nebraska Press: Nebraska: 2009

BROWN, DEE, *Bury My Heart at Wounded Knee*, Barrie & Jenkins: London: 1970

The Fetterman Massacre, Barrie & Jenkins: London: 1972

Brown, JOSEPH E., *The Sacred Pipe*, Penguin Books: Baltimore: 1971

BROWN, MARK H., *The Plainsmen of the Yellowstone*, Putnam: New York: 1961

BRUST, JAMES S., *Where Custer Fell,* University of Oklahoma Press: Oklahoma: 2005

BURT, MARY E., *The Boy General*, Charles Scribner & Sons: New York: 1941

CAPPS, BENJAMIN, *The Great Chiefs*, Time-Life Books: New York: 1974

The Indians, Time-Life books: New York: 1976

CARROLL, JOHN M., *The Benteen – Goldin Letters*, University of Nebraska Press: Nebraska: 1991

They Rode With Custer, J.M. Carroll & Co.: New York: 1993

CATLIN, GEORGE, *North American Indians*, Penguin Books: London: 1989

CHAMBERS, LEE, *Fort Abraham Lincoln, Dakota Territory*, Schiffer Books: Atglen: 2008

CHUN, CLAYTON S., *U.S. Army in the Plains Indian Wars*, Osprey Publishing: Oxford: 2004

CLARK, W.P. (Captain), I*ndian Sign Language*, Hamersly & Co.: Philadelphia: 1885

CODY, IRON EYES, *Indian Talk,* New English Library: London: 1972

COHAN SCHERER, J., *Indians*, Octopus Books: London: 1974

COLLIER, JOHN, *Indians of the Americas*, New American Library: New York: 1964

COLLINS, J.S., *Across the Plains in '64*, Nebraska: 1904

CONNELL, EVEN S., *Son of the Morning Star*, Book Club Association: London: 1985

COX, KURT H., *Custer and His Commands*, Greenhill Books: London: 1999

COZZENS, PETER, *The Earth Is Weeping*, Atlantic Books: London: 2016

CROOK, GEORGE (General), *Autobiography*, University of Oklahoma Press: Oklahoma: 1946

CURTIS, EDWARD S., *Native Americans*, Taschen: London: 2001

CURTIS, NATALIE, *The Indian Book*, Harper & Bros: New York: 1907

CUSTER, ELIZABETH, *Boots and Saddles*, University of Oklahoma Press: Oklahoma: 1968

Following the Guidon, University of Nebraska Press: Nebraska: 1994

Tenting On The Plains, University of Oklahoma Press: Oklahoma: 1982

CUSTER, GEORGE A. (Lieutenant Colonel), *My Life on the Plains*, W.H. Allen & Co. Ltd: London: 1982

The Custer Story (Letters of G.A. & Elizabeth), Devin-Adair: New York: 1950

DARLING, ROGER, *General Custer's Final Hours*, Potomac-Western Press: Virginia: 1992

DE BARTHE, JOSEPH, *Life and Adventures of Frank Grouard*, The Buffalo Bulletin: 1894

DE LAND, CHARLES, *The Sioux wars,* South Dakota historical Collection: Vol.15: 1930

DELORIA Jnr, VINE, *Behind the Trail of Broken Treaties*, University of Texas: Texas: 1985

Custer Died for your Sins, Macmillan Publishing: New York: 1969

DILLON, RICHARD H., *North American Indian Wars*, Magna Books: Wigston : 1983

DIPPIE, BRIAN W., *Custer's Last Stand,* University of Montana Publications: Montana: 1976

DODGE, RICHARD (Colonel), *The Hunting Grounds of the Great West*, 1877

DONOVAN, JAMES, *A Terrible Glory*, Little, Brown & Co.: London: 2008

Custer and the Little Big Horn, Crestline: New York: 2001

DU BOIS, CHARLES G., *Kick the dead Lion*, The Reporter printing & Supply Co.: Billings: 1961

DUNN, J.P., *Massacres of the Mountains*, New York: 1886

DUSTIN, FRED, *The Custer Tragedy*, 1939

EASTERWOOD, T.J., *Memories of Seventy-Six,* New York Herald: 1876

EDGERLY, WINFIELD S., *Narrative of the March of Gen. G.A. Custer*, Ghent Papers: Washington

FARB, PETER, *Man's Rise to Civilisation*, Granada Publishing Ltd: London: 1971

FEHRENBACH, T.R., *Comanches,* Pimlico: London: 1974

FELTON, MARK, *Today Is A Good Day To Fight*, The History Press: Stroud: 2009

FIELD, RON, *Forts of the American Frontier 1820 – 91*, Osprey Publishing: Oxford: 2005

U.S. Army Frontier Scouts, Osprey Publishing: Oxford: 2003

FOUGERE, KATHERINE, *With Custer's cavalry*, The Caxton Printers: Idaho: 1940

FOX, RED (Chief), *The Memories of Chief Red Fox*, W.H. Allen: London: 1971

FROST, LAWRENCE A., *Custer Victorious*, University of Nebraska Press: Nebraska: 1990

The Court Martial of Gen. G.A. Custer, University of Oklahoma Press: Oklahoma: 1987

GARLAND, HAMLIN, *General Custer's Last Fight as Seen by Two Moon*, McClure's Magazine Vol 11: 1898

GARST, SHANNON, *Crazy Horse, A Great Warrior of the Sioux*, 1950

GHENT, WILLIAM J., *Accounts of the Custer Fight given to General Hugh Scott by two Crow Scouts, 'White Man Runs Him' and 'Curley', August 24th 1919,* Ghent Papers: Library of Congress: Washington

Criticism of Godfrey's Custer Article, U.S. Army Military History Institute, Carlisle Barracks: Pennsylvania

Criticism of Murray's Custer Article, U.S. Army Military History Institute, Carlisle barracks: Pennsylvania

GIBBON, GUY, *The Sioux*, Blackwell Publishing: Malden: 1970

GIBBON, JOHN (Colonel), *Gibbon On The Sioux Campaign of 1876*, The Old Army Press: Nebraska: 1970

GIDLEY, M., *With One Sky Above Us*, Webb & Bower Books: Leicester: 1979

GOBLE, PAUL, *Red Hawk's Account of Custer's Last Battle*, Brigham: Utah: 1976

GODFREY, EDWARD S., *Address at the Custer Battlefield on the 40th Anniversary of the Battle*, Parmly Billings Library: Billings

Custer's Last Battle, Century Magazine: January 1892

Diary of Captain E.S. Godfrey: Battle if the Little Big Horn 1876, Ghent: Papers: Washington

Letter to Major C.H. Asbury 18 – 1 – 1929, Eastern Montana College: Billings

The death of General Custer, The Cavalry Journal Vol. XXXVI: July 1927

Voluminous Material Covering all of his Military Life, Military Research Collection, Carlisle Barracks: Pennsylvania

GOLDIN, THEODORE, *Battle of the Little Big Horn: Securing water*, U.S. Military History Institute: Carlisle barracks: Pennsylvania

GOODRICH, THOMAS, *Scalp Dance*, Stackpole Books: Mechanicsburg: 1995

GRAHAM, W.A., *The Custer Myth*, Stackpole Books: Mechanicsburg: 1995

The Lost Is Found: Custer's Last Message Comes To Light, The cavalry Journal Vol. LI: 1942

The Reno Court of Inquiry, Stackpole Books: Mechanicsburg: 1995

The Story of the Little Big Horn, Stackpole Books: Mechanicsburg: 1994

GRAY, JOHM S., *Centennial Campaign of the Sioux War 1876*, University of Oklahoma Press: Oklahoma: 1988

Custer's Last Campaign, University of Nebraska Press: Lincoln: 1991

GREENE, JEROME A., *Evidence of the Custer Enigma*, Outbooks: Reno: 1979

Indian War Veterans, Savas Beattie LLC: New York: 2007

Slim Buttes 1876, University of Oklahoma Press: Oklahoma: 1891

GRINNEL, GEORGE B., *The Cheyenne Indians*, Yale University Press: New haven: 1923

The Fighting Cheyennes, University of Oklahoma Press: Oklahoma: 1956

GURNEY, GENE, *The Pictorial history of the U.S. Army*, New York: 1966

GWYNNE, S.C., *Empire of the Summer Moon*, Constable & Robinson: London: 2011

HAGEMANN, E.R., *Fighting Rebels and Redskins*, University of Oklahoma Press: Oklahoma: 1969

HAMMER, KENNETH, *Custer in '76*, Walter Camp's Notes on the Custer Fight, Brigham: Utah: 1976

Men With Custer, The Old Army Press: 1972

HARDORFF, RICHARD G., *Cheyenne Memories of the Custer Fight*, University of Nebraska Press: Lincoln: 1998

Lakota Recollections of the Custer Fight, University of Nebraska Press: Lincoln: 1997

HATCH, TOM, *The Custer Companion*, Stackpole Books: Mechanicsburg: 2002

HEDREN, PAUL L., *We Trailed the Sioux*, Stackpole Books: Mechanicsburg: 2003

HENRY, WILL, *Custer's last stand*, G & D: 1968

HOEBEL, E. ADAMSON, *The Cheyennes*, Holt, Rinehart & Winston Inc: New York: 1960

HOIG, STAN, *The Sand Creek Massacre*, University of Oklahoma Press: Oklahoma: 1961

HOOK, JASON, *American Plains Indians,* Osprey Publishing: Oxford: 1985

The Apaches, Osprey Publishing: Oxford: 1987

HOOK, RICHARD, *Warriors at the Little Big Horn 1876*, Osprey Publishing: Oxford: 2004

HOWARD, O.O., *My Life and Experiences Among the Hostile Indians*, Hartford: 1907

HUGHES, HOWARD, *The American Indian Wars*, Pocket Essentials: Herts: 2001

HUMFREVILLE, J. LEE, *Twenty Years Among Our Hostile Indians*, Hunter & Co.: New York: 1903

HUMPHREYS MILLER, D., *Custer's Fall*, Transworld Publishers: London: 1965

HUNT, BRIAN V., *Reno Court of Inquiry*, Big Byte Books: 2015

HUNT, FRAZIER, *Custer, Last of the cavaliers*, Cosmopolitan Book Corp.: New York: 1928

HUTCHINS, JAMES, *7th U.S. Cavalry 1876*, Military Collector & Historian: Vol. X No.4: Winter 1958

HYDE, GEORGE E., *A Sioux Chronicle*, University of Oklahoma Press: Oklahoma: 1980

Indians of the High Plains, 1959

Red Cloud's Folk, University of Oklahoma Press; Oklahoma: 1961

Spotted Tail's Folk, University of Oklahoma Press: Oklahoma: 1961

JACKSON, DONALD, *Custer's Gold: U.S. Cavalry Expedition of 1874*, Yale University Press: Yale: 1967

JOHNSON, ERIC S., *No Greater Calling*, Schiffer Publishing: Atglen: 2012

JOHNSON, MICHAEL, *The Native Tribes of North America*, Compendium Publishing: London: 1999

Tribes of the Sioux nation, Osprey Publishing: Oxford: 2000

JOHNSON, SWAFFORD, *History of the U.S. Cavalry*, Hamlyn: London: 1985

JONES, DOUGLAS C., *The Court Martial of George A. Custer*, Scribner: New Jersey: 1964

JOSEPHY Jnr, ALVIN M., *500 Nations*, Alfred A Knope: New York: 1994

KATCHER, PHILIP, *The American Indian Wars 1860 – 1890*, Osprey Publishing: Oxford: 1995

U.S. Cavalry on the Plains 1850 – 90, Osprey Publishing: Oxford: 1995

KERRIGAN, EVANS E., *American War Medals & Decorations*, Viking Press: New York: 1964

KERSHAW, ROBERT J., *Red Sabbath*, Ian Allan Publishing: Hersham: 2006

KIDD, J.H., *Personal Recollections of a Cavalrymen*, Sentinel Printing Co.: 1908

KING, CHARLES, *Campaigning with Crook*, New York: 1890

KLOKNER, JAMES B., *The Officer Corps of Custer's Seventh Cavalry*, Schiffer Military History: Atglen: 2007

KOSTER, JOHN, Chronology Books: New York: 2010

KUHLMAN, CHARLES, *Legend into History*, Stackpole Books: Mechanicsburg: 1952

LA FORGE, OLIVER, *A Pictorial History of the American Indian*, Spring Books: London: 1966

LANGELLIER, JOHN P., *Bluecoats*, Greenhill Books: London: 1995

Longknives, Greenhill Books: London: 1996

LAVENDER, DAVID, *The Penguin Book of the American West*, Longman's: London: 1969

LECKIE, WILLIAM H., *Military Conquest of the Southern Plains*, University of Oklahoma Press: Oklahoma: 1963

LIBBY, ORIN G., *The Arikara Narrative of Custer's Campaign & the Battle of the Little Big Horn*, University of Oklahoma Press: Oklahoma: 1998

LONGSTREET, STEPHEN, *War Cries On Horseback*, W.H. Allen: London: 1970

LUCE, EDWARD, *Custer Battlefield National Monument, National Park Service Historical Handbook Series 1*, Washington Government Printing Office:1949

McCHRISTIAN, DOUGLAS C., *The U.S. Army in the west 1870 -1880*, University of Oklahoma Press: Oklahoma: 1995

McCLERNAND, EDWARD, *The Indian and the Buffalo in Montana*, The Cavalry Journal: January 1927

McCRACKEN, HAROLD, *George Catlin and the Old Frontier*, Bonanza Books: New York: 1959

McGINNIS, ANTHONY R., *Counting Coup and Cutting Horses*, University of Nebraska Press: Nebraska: 2010

McLUHAN, T.C., *Touch The earth*, Sphere Books: London: 1972

MACLEAN, FRENCH L. (Colonel), *Custer's Best*, Schiffer Military History: Atglen: 2011

MAGNUSSEN, DANIEL, *Thompson's Narrative of the Little Big Horn 1876*, A.H. Clark: California: 1974

MALLERY, GARRICK (Colonel), *Gesture Signs and Signals of the North American Indian,* Bureau of American Ethnology: Smithsonian Institute: Washington: 1881

MANCHIP WHITE, JON, *Everyday Life of the North American Indian*, Batsford: London: 1979

MARQUIS, THOMAS, *Custer and the Little Big Horn*, 1969

Keep the Last Bullet for Yourself, Two Centuries Publishing: New York: 1976

Wooden Leg: A Warrior Who Fought Custer, University of Nebraska Press: Nebraska: 1957

MARSHALL III, JOSEPH M., *The Day The World Ended*, Penguin Books: London: 2008

MEED, DOUGLAS V., *Comanche 1800 – 74,* Osprey Publishing: Oxford: 2003

MERRINGTON, MARQUERITE, *The Life of General George Armstrong Custer*, University of Nebraska Press: Nebraska: 1971

MEYER, ROY W., *History of the Santee Sioux*, University of Nebraska Press: Nebraska: 1967

MICHINO, GREGORY F., *Forgotten Fights*, Mountain Press Publishers Co.: Montana: 2008

Lakota Noon, Mountain Press Publisher Co.: Montana: 2007

The Mystery of E Troop, Mountain Press Publisher Co.: Montana: 2005

MILES, NELSON A. (General), *Personal Recollections*, 1897

MILLS, ANSON, *My Story*, Washington: 1918

MILLS, CHARLES K., *Harvest of Barren Regrets*, University of Nebraska Press: Nebraska: 2011

MONNETT, JOHN H., *Where a Hundred Soldiers were Killed*, University of New Mexico Press: Albuquerque: 2010

MOONEY, JAMES, *The Ghost Dance*, J.G. Press: USA

MOORE, JOHN H., *The Cheyenne*, Blackwell Publishers: Oxford: 1996

MOORE, MARIJO, *Eating Fire, Tasting Blood*, Running Press Book Publishers: Philadelphia: 2006

MOQUIN, WAYNE, *Great Documents in American Indian History*, Da Capo Press: New York: 1973

MORRIS, JAMES M., *History of the U.S. Army*, Bison Books: London: 1986

NEIHARDT, JOHN G., *Black Elk Speaks*, Sphere Books: London: 1974

NEVIN, DAVID, *The Soldiers*, Time-Life Books: New York: 1974

NICHOLS, RONALD H., *In Custer's Shadow*, University of Oklahoma Press: Oklahoma: 2000

Men With Custer, Custer Battlefield Hist. & Museum Assoc. Inc: Montana: 2000

OGDEN, H.A., *Uniforms of the United States Army 1774 – 1889*, Dover Publications: New York: 1998

OLSON, JAMES C., *Red Cloud and the Sioux Problem*, University of Nebraska Press: Nebraska: 1965

OVERFIELD II, LOYD J., *The Little Big Horn 1876*, University of Nebraska Press: Nebraska: 1990

PANZERI, PETER, *Little Big Horn 1876*, Osprey Publishing: Oxford: 1995

PARKS, JACK, *Custer,* Nordon Publications: New York: 1975

PARSONS, JOHN E., *Firearms In The Custer Battle*, Stackpole: Harrisburg: 1953

PEGLER, MARTIN, *U.S. Cavalryman 1865 – 1890*, Osprey Publications: Oxford: 1993

PHILBRICK, NATHANIEL, *The Last Stand*, The Bodley Head: London: 2010

RED FOX, *The Memoires of Chief Red Fox*, W.H. Allen: London: 1971

REEDSTROM, E. LISLE, *Custer's 7th Cavalry*, Sterling Publishing Co. Inc.: New York: 1992

REYNOLDS, QUENTIN, *Custer's Last Stand*, Random House: New York: 1952

RICKER, ELI S., *Voices of the American West Vol 1: The Indian Interviews*, University of Nebraska Press: Nebraska: 2005

Voices of the American West Vol 2: The settler & Soldier Interviews, University of Nebraska Press : Nebraska: 2005

ROBERTS, DAVID, *Once They Moved Like the wind*, Pimlico: London: 1998

ROBINSON III, CHARLES M., *The Plains Wars*, Osprey Publishing: Oxford: 2003

ROBINSON, DOANE, *Crazy Horse's Story of the Custer Battle*, South Dakota Historical Collection Vol 6: 1912

ROSENBURG, BRUCE, *Custer and the Epic Defeat*, Penn. State University Press: 1974

ROWLAND, WILLIS, *The Story of White Elk as Told to Willis Rowland at Lame Deer, Montana May 25th 1927*: Billings Library: Montana

RUSSELL, DON, *Custer's Last Stand,* Abram's: New York: 1971

RUTLEDGE, LEE A., *Field Uniforms of the Indian Wars Army 1866 – 1871*, North Cape Publications: California: 1998

Field Uniforms of the Indian Wars army 1872 – 1886, North Cape Publications: California: 1997

SANDOZ, MARI, *Cheyenne Autumn*, Eye & Spottiswood: London: 1966

Crazy Horse, the Strange Man of the Oglalas, Knopf: New York: 1945

Hostiles and Friendlies, University of Nebraska Press; Nebraska: 1959

The Battle of the Little Big Horn, J.B. Lippincott Co.: New York: 1966

SCHERA, JOANNA COHAN, *Indians*, Octopus Books: London: 1974

SCHMECKBIER, LAWRENCE E., *The Office of Indian Affairs*, John Hopkins Press: Baltimore: 1927

SCHMITT, MARTIN F., *General George Crook*, University of Oklahoma Press: Oklahoma: 1986

Fighting Indians of the West, Bonanza Books: New York: 1948

SCOTT, DOUGLAS, *They Died With Custer*, University of Oklahoma Press: Oklahoma: 1998

SCRUDDER, RALPH, *Custer Country*, Binford: Oregan: 1963

SELBY, JOHN, *U.S. Cavalry*, Osprey Publications: Oxford: 1972

SETON, EARNEST T., *Sign Talk*, Doubleday: New York: 1918

SEYMOUR, FLORA W., *Indian Agents of the Old Frontier*, Appleton-Century: New York: 1941

SPENCE, LEWIS, *Myths & Legends of the North American Indians*, Parragon: Bristol: 1998

STEVENSON, JOAN N., *Deliverance from the Little Big Horn*, University of Oklahoma Press: Oklahoma: 2012

STEWART, EDGAR, *Custer's Luck*, University of Oklahoma Press: Oklahoma: 1955

Penny-an-Acre Empire in the West, University of Oklahoma Press: Oklahoma: 1968

STILES, T.J., *Custer Trials*, Vintage Books: 2016

TAYLOR, COLIN, *The Native Americans*, Salamander Books: London: 2000

The Plains Indians, Salamander Books: London: 1994

The warriors of the Plains, Hamlyn publishing: London: 1975

TAYLOR, WILLIAM O., *With Custer on the Little Big Horn*, Penguin Group: London: 1996

TILLET, LESLIE, *Wind on the Buffalo Grass*, Crowell: New York: 1976

TUCKER, PHILLIP, *Why Custer was Never Warned*, Universal Publishers: Irvine: 2017

TURNER, DON, *Custer's First Massacre*, Humbly Gulch Press: Texas: 1968

URWIN, GREGORY J.W., *The United States cavalry*, Blandford Press: London: 1985

The United States Infantry, Blandford Press: London: 1988

UTLEY, ROBERT M, *Bluecoats and Redskins*, Purnell Books: London: 1975

Cavalier In Buckskin, Salamander Books: London: 2001

Custer and the Great Controversy, Westernlore: Los Angeles: 1962

Custer Battlefield National Monument, Dept. of the Interior: Washington: 1969

Frontiersmen in Blue, Macmillan: New York: 1967

Life In Custer's cavalry, University of Nebraska Press: Nebraska: 1987

The Last Days of the Sioux Nation, Yale University Press: 1963

VAN DE WATER, FREDERIC, *Glory Hunter*, Bobbs-Merrill Co.: Indianapolis: 1934

VAUGHAN, J.W., *With Crook at the Rosebud*, Stackpole: Harrisburg: 1956

VESTAL, STANLEY, *Sitting Bull*, University of Oklahoma Press: Oklahoma: 1857

Warpath, Houghton Mifflin: Boston: 1834

VIOLA, HERMAN J., *Is It A Good Day To Die*, University of Nebraska Press: Nebraska: 2001

Trail to Wounded Knee, National Geographic: Washington: 2003

WALKER, J.R., *The Sun Dance and Other Ceremonies of the Teton Dakota*, Forgotten Books: UK: 2008

WELCH, JAMES, *Killing Custer*, W.W. Norton & Co. Inc.: New York: 1994

WELSH, WILLIAM, *Report and Supplement Report of a Visit to Spotted Tail's Tribe of Brule Sioux Indians*, Philadelphia: 1870

WHITE BULL, JOSEPH, *The warrior Who Killed Custer*, University of Nebraska Press: Nebraska: 1968

WHITTAKER, FREDERICK, *A Complete Life of General George A. Custer*, Sheldon & Co.: New York: 1876

WILLIAMS, ROGER L., *Military Register of Custer's Last Command*, University of Oklahoma Press: Oklahoma: 2012

WINDOLPH, CHARLES, *I Fought With Custer*, University of Nebraska Press; Nebraska: 1974

WINDROW, MARTIN, *Military dress of North America 1665 – 1970*, Ian Allan: London: 1973

WOOD, NORMAN B., *Lives of Famous Indian Chiefs*, American Indian Historical Pub. Vo.: Illinois: 1906

YENNE, BELL, *Indian Wars*, Westholme Publishing: 2006

ZIMMERMAN, LARRY J., *American Indians: the First Nations,* Duncan Baird Pub: London: 2003

U.S. GOVERNMENT PAPERS

Index to Reports of Committees of the House of Representatives for the 1st Session: 44th Congress: 1875 – 1876

Report on the Material Wealth, Climate and Rainfall and Natural Resources of the Black Hills of South Dakota: 1st Session: 44th Congress: Exec. Doc 51

Report of the Commissioner of Indian Affairs in Relation to the Present Situation of Indian Disturbances in the Sioux Reservations: 1st Session: 44th Congress: Sen. Doc. 52

Indian Affairs, Laws and Treaties 1 – 11: 1st Session: 57th Congress; Sen. Exec. Doc. 452 (3)

2nd Session: 62nd Congress: Sen. Exec> Doc 719

Report of the Expedition to the Black Hills under the command of Brevet Major General G.A. Custer: 2nd Session: 43rd Congress: Sen. Exec>Doc. 32

Report of the Secretary of War – Communicated to the Two Houses of Congress at the beginning of the 2nd session: 45th Congress: Vol. II Part II: 1876/1877

United States War Department Report on the Military Expedition Against the Sioux Indians: Report July 14th 1876: 1st Session: 44th Congress: House Exec. Doc. 184

United States War Department Report 1876: 2nd Session: 44th Congress: House Exec. Doc. I Part II

2nd Session 44th Congress: Sen. Exec. Doc 9

Discussions of H.R. 1335 (X192: 44/1 and X197: 44/1): 2nd session: 44th Congress

LIST OF Killed and Wounded in Action with Sioux, Little Big Horn River, Montana: Official Army List of 1876: National Archives; Washington

Medal of Honor Recipients 1863 -1978: Sen. Comm. Print No 3.:
National Archives, Washington
Transcript of the Reno Court of Inquiry 1878/1879
National Archives Micro. Pub. M – 592: Rolls 1 and 2
National Archives: Washington

U.S. GOVERNMENT PUBLICATIONS

Cavalry equipment 1874
Custer Battlefield 1961
Custer Battlefield 1969
Entrenchment Trail: Custer Battlefield
Horse Equipments & Cavalry Accoutrements 1891
Horse Equipments & Equipments for Officers and Enlisted men 1905
U.S. Army Uniforms and Equipment 1889

Index